A CONTEMPORARY VERSION
OF THE 'BOOK OF PROVERBS'
WITH LEADERSHIP INSIGHTS

77 PROVERBS
FOR LEADERS

MARK BILTON

A Monday Matters
Publication

"Often the last place that leaders think of going for business insights is ... the Bible. And yet, it is cram-packed full of brilliant leadership principles and practice. In this latest book, Mark Bilton draws fresh, relevant and contemporary business wisdom, from that old, old book in the most amazing way. A must read."

BERNI DYMET, INTERNATIONAL RADIO PERSONALITY, AUTHOR, SPEAKER AND CEO CHRISTIANITY WORKS.

"When you meet and know Mark, you then understand his success revolves around the input and wisdom he has practiced from the Book Of Proverbs. What a great way to read, learn and grow from the words God spoke through His people."

PETER IRVINE, CO FOUNDER GLORIA JEAN'S COFFEES AUSTRALIA, AUTHOR AND SPEAKER.

"I often read the Proverbs sequentially to begin my day with the wisdom of God. Each chapter contains a healthy call to all of us to live in the perspective only the Holy Spirit can provide. Now, Mark Bilton connects each Proverb to a concrete business question or challenge. What a gift to the followers of Jesus seeking to live out their faith in the marketplace!"

MIKE BAER, CHIEF PEOPLE OFFICER, EMPLOYBRIDGE USA, INTERNATIONAL SPEAKER AND AUTHOR OF 'BUSINESS AS MISSION'.

"Wisdom is the principal thing. Therefore get wisdom ...." 77 Proverbs for Leaders by Mark Bilton amazingly draws on and elucidates, powerful statements from one of the most insightful writers of all time. The writer of Proverbs laid out things that God actually imparted to him. His reign was Israel's most glorious. When you have wisdom you see and know what God sees and knows. Therefore get into 77 Proverbs ... and get wisdom!"

TONY MCLENNAN, CEO BIBLE LEAGUE AUSTRALIA AND NEW ZEALAND.

"In '77 Proverbs for Leaders', I think Mark is on to the greatest principle of building Kingdom success. This book will help many with the practical application of the wisdom and understanding of God in their daily lives and occupations, and truly inspire, challenge and equip people in fulfilling their Kingdom purpose."

DR. SEAN MORRIS, SENIOR PASTOR GROW INC.

"Learn from someone who has walked the walk, not just talks the talk. Mark is a rare breed of new leader who can successfully integrate both work and faith. Mark's teaching is needed now more than ever".

ALEX COOK, FOUNDER AND EXECUTIVE DIRECTOR, WEALTH WITH PURPOSE.

"What a read! A God inspired book written by a man of integrity who has truly "walked the walk" in business for many years."

STEVEN P BENNETT OAM, FOUNDER, BENBRO ELECTRONICS, AND AUTHOR OF 'MORE THAN A CONQUEROR'.

"In 77 Proverbs, Mark takes us on the simple yet profound journey from knowledge to wisdom. Mark shares freely from his own experiences in the marketplace and from his perspective as a business leader - a must read for those among us who desire God's promised 'hidden treasure'."

JOSHUA JAGELMAN, CHAIRMAN, INTEGRITY SERVICES GLOBAL, DIRECTOR, YUNNAN COFFEE TRADERS, AND GENERAL MANAGER, JAGELMAN KINAHAN CONSULTANTS.

Called to Business
19 Delaware Avenue,
St Ives NSW 2075 AUSTRALIA
Telephone +61 2 99880956
www.CalledtoBusiness.com

In association with:

Ark House Press
PO Box 1722, Port Orchard, WA 98366 USA
PO Box 1321, Mona Vale NSW 1660 Australia
PO Box 318 334, West Harbour, Auckland 0661 New Zealand
arkhousepress.com

Except where otherwise indicated in the text, the Scripture quotations contained
herein are from 'The World Edition Bible' (WEB) an updated version of the
'American Standard Version' 1901. For the sake of common understanding God's
name 'Yahweh' has been translated as 'the LORD'.

Cataloguing in Publication Data:
Title: 77 PROVERBS for Leaders. A Contemporary Version of the 'Book of Proverbs'
with Leadership Insights. / Mark Bilton
ISBN: 9780994235206 (paperback)
ISBN: 9780994235213 (ebook)
Subjects: Religion and Theology, Business and Economic
Dewey Number: 248.4

Cover & Layout by Justine Elliott – Book Layout Guru

My son, if you will receive my words,

and store up my commandments within you;

So as to turn your ear to wisdom,

and apply your heart to understanding;

Yes, if you call out for discernment,

and lift up your voice for understanding;

If you seek her as silver,

and search for her as for hidden treasures:

then you will understand the fear of the LORD,

and find the knowledge of God.

PROVERBS CHAPTER 2, VERSES 1-5.

CONTENTS

ACKNOWLEDGEMENTS

Proverbs is the Book of Wisdom. Wisdom is based on a respect for God. He is Wisdom, He is Knowledge, He is Grace, He is Mercy, He is Peace, and He is Love. To my Lord and Saviour Jesus Christ, without whom I have neither wisdom, knowledge, mercy, peace, grace nor love.

INTRODUCTION

I love 'The Book of Proverbs'! It is a seemingly unending source of knowledge and understanding. It is literally infused with the knowledge and mind of God. Its message of wisdom is available to all who will come and hear it's eternal truth.

'Proverbs' is a book in the Bible that has been venerated by Jews, Christians and secular commentators alike. It's anchor is the belief that the 'fear of' (meaning 'submission to') God, is the beginning of all wisdom. King Solomon, the most renown the it's writers has become synonymous with wisdom. He was reputedly one of the wisest and wealthiest people in history and was and is widely admired.

'Proverbs' whilst largely attributed to Solomon also contains writings from the historically mysterious King Lempel and Agur.

Truth in Proverbs is occasionally, as in life, the tension between two seemingly contradictory positions. It is not simply a prescriptive list of required behaviours, but encourages the reader to explore and go deeper, to better understand its meaning. Inspired by God it compels the reader to seek God's revelation to get to the real meaning under some of the complexity and seeming contradiction.

At other times Proverbs lays it out in black and white, cuts through the temporal situational complexity and speaks in absolutes; Simple clarity from the 'Throne of Grace' to those who, with child like faith, will be obedient to the call and surrender to the will and wisdom of God.

Godly wisdom is timeless. At its core are principals and revelation that are laid down in the very fabric of our existence. God's wisdom is often seen as foolish to man, counter intuitive and even outmoded. Yet it has remained as the fundamental basis of fulfillment, destiny and purpose as it is accessed and expressed through our relationship with Him.

If you are a 'leader' or aspire to be one, you need wisdom. This is how you get it. Read it! Then live it! Proverbs contains some of the most applicable nuggets of truth in the entire Bible. God reveals the practical and the miniscule in the midst of the big picture. Proverbs is accessible and practical in its application to the everyday in our every day.

I have chosen to highlight '77 Proverbs' and expound from my own leadership experience of how I have endeavoured to apply these ancient sayings in my work place. God's wisdom is timeless, God bless you as you trust Him and serve Him in your workplace.

THE BOOK OF
PROVERBS

CHAPTER 1

The proverbs of Solomon, the son of David, king of Israel:
to know wisdom and instruction;
to discern the words of understanding;
to receive instruction in wise dealing,
in righteousness, justice, and equity;
to give prudence to the simple,
knowledge and discretion to the young man:
that the wise man may hear, and increase in learning;
that the man of understanding may attain to sound counsel:
to understand a proverb, and parables,
the words and riddles of the wise.

The fear of the LORD is the beginning of knowledge;
but the foolish despise wisdom and instruction.
My son, listen to your father's instruction,
and don't forsake your mother's teaching:
for they will be a garland to grace your head,
and chains around your neck.
My son, if sinners entice you, don't consent.
If they say, "Come with us,
Let's lay in wait for blood;
let's lurk secretly for the innocent without cause;
let's swallow them up alive like Sheol,
and whole, like those who go down into the pit.
We'll find all valuable wealth.
We'll fill our houses with spoil.
You shall cast your lot among us.
We'll all have one purse."

ONE

KNOWLEDGE

> *"The fear of the LORD is the beginning of knowledge; but the foolish despise wisdom and instruction.* (PRO 1:7)

What is knowledge? Is it just the accumulation of facts or something deeper? In my view, it needs to be applicable to have any value. The fear of God is described as the beginning of knowledge, the foundation of understanding. This is not just some ethereal understanding of God but a practical knowledge that is applicable in the real world, in our everyday existence at work.

As leaders we will be stretched by the challenges that our positions inevitably provide. But we are assured we will not be stretched beyond our ability to bear and that His yoke is easy. However, we need His wisdom to discern and get insight.

If wisdom is to develop, we need to know that God is God and that His Word is revelation. If you want knowledge, go to God, read His Word, and ask His Spirit to reveal its treasures to you. Do this and you will have knowledge, instruction, and wisdom.

> **QUICK PRAYER**: Help me to respect Your Word for Your sake. Amen.

My son, don't walk in the way with them.

Keep your foot from their path,

for their feet run to evil.

They hurry to shed blood.

For in vain is the net spread in the sight of any bird:

but these lay wait for their own blood.

They lurk secretly for their own lives.

So are the ways of everyone who is greedy for gain.

It takes away the life of its owners.

Wisdom calls aloud in the street.

She utters her voice in the public squares.

She calls at the head of noisy places.

At the entrance of the city gates, she utters her words:

"How long, you simple ones, will you love simplicity?

How long will mockers delight themselves in mockery,

and fools hate knowledge?

Turn at my reproof.

Behold, I will pour out my spirit on you.

I will make known my words to you.

Because I have called, and you have refused;

I have stretched out my hand, and no one has paid attention;

but you have ignored all my counsel,

and wanted none of my reproof;

I also will laugh at your disaster.

I will mock when calamity overtakes you;

when calamity overtakes you like a storm,

when your disaster comes on like a whirlwind;

MARKETING

"For in vain is the net spread in the sight of any bird:" (PRO 1:17)

We live in a world that is saturated with overt marketing and an information highway driven by social media. Blatant marketing is now receiving the disdain of educated and critical consumers. We need to be much smarter in how we present our products in a desirable light.

Influencing the influencers, experiential marketing, social responsibility, and alignment with good causes are all good ways to target marketing without shouting about the brand and getting a negative response.

There has never been a time when resources to target the individual have been in such abundance. We can now literally market to a target of one.

If you want to be really creative, how about asking the Creator? In Him are the fullness of creativity and the fullness of wisdom. What an indescribable resource.

> **QUICK PRAYER**: Please fill me with your wisdom and strategies. Amen.

when distress and anguish come on you.

Then will they call on me, but I will not answer.

They will seek me diligently, but they will not find me;

because they hated knowledge,

and didn't choose the fear of the LORD.

They wanted none of my counsel.

They despised all my reproof.

Therefore they will eat of the fruit of their own way,

and be filled with their own schemes.

For the backsliding of the simple will kill them.

The careless ease of fools will destroy them.

But whoever listens to me will dwell securely,

and will be at ease, without fear of harm."

THREE

REBUKE

> *"Turn at my reproof. Behold, I will pour out my spirit on you. I will make known my words to you"* (PRO 1:23)

Regardless of our position we are all responsible to someone. Even as a business owner you have the ultimate arbiter of your success, your customer.

I hate discipline. When God is working on something in my life, those adjustments are sometimes not easy. However, as we respond to those things, God begins to talk to us, reveal more of Himself, and make known more of His character and ways. Sometimes we miss out on His blessings because we resist His correction.

These corrections are always for a purpose. He will often highlight a behavior because it may well cause us to stumble down the track. He doesn't do it for His entertainment but for our greater good.

His promise is to "pour out His thoughts." Imagine that—thinking the thoughts of God.

QUICK PRAYER: Thank You that there is wisdom after a rebuke. Amen.

CHAPTER 2

My son, if you will receive my words,
and store up my commandments within you;
So as to turn your ear to wisdom,
and apply your heart to understanding;
Yes, if you call out for discernment,
and lift up your voice for understanding;
If you seek her as silver,
and search for her as for hidden treasures:
then you will understand the fear of the LORD,
and find the knowledge of God.
For the LORD gives wisdom.
Out of his mouth comes knowledge and understanding.
He lays up sound wisdom for the upright.
He is a shield to those who walk in integrity;
that he may guard the paths of justice,
and preserve the way of his saints.
Then you will understand righteousness and justice,
equity and every good path.
For wisdom will enter into your heart.
Knowledge will be pleasant to your soul.
Discretion will watch over you.
Understanding will keep you,
to deliver you from the way of evil,
from the men who speak perverse things;
who forsake the paths of uprightness,
to walk in the ways of darkness;
who rejoice to do evil,
and delight in the perverseness of evil;

FOUR

INSIGHT

> *"If you seek her as silver, and search for*
> *her as for hidden treasures: then you will*
> *understand the fear of the LORD, and*
> *find the knowledge of God."* (PRO 2:3–5)

Imagine the smartest guys in the world all in the same room—the business world's who's who. Buffet, Jobs, Gates, Morgan, whoever you want. You have absolute access. How exciting would that be?

We have access to a mind, an understanding, a power of change, and a foreseer of all with an infinite capacity and all the time and individual attention we want. Yet sometimes we lose the comprehension of such access. It cost a lot—more than money can buy. Let's not take it for granted.

There is an essence in the Scripture that understanding and wisdom need to be toiled for, as searching for gold or silver. There is a measure of discipline, sweat, dedication, and work required. Will we pay the price for insight beyond our realm of understanding? Will we seek the wisdom of God? Wow, what a privilege to have access to the throne room of unfathomable grace.

> **QUICK PRAYER:** Please give me insight into those things that prevail against me. Amen.

who are crooked in their ways,

and wayward in their paths:

To deliver you from the strange woman,

even from the foreigner who flatters with her words;

who forsakes the friend of her youth,

and forgets the covenant of her God:

for her house leads down to death,

her paths to the dead.

None who go to her return again,

neither do they attain to the paths of life:

that you may walk in the way of good men,

and keep the paths of the righteous.

For the upright will dwell in the land.

The perfect will remain in it.

But the wicked will be cut off from the land.

The treacherous will be rooted out of it.

FIVE

PLEASANT KNOWLEDGE

> *"For wisdom will enter into your heart.*
> *Knowledge will be pleasant to your*
> *soul. Discretion will watch over you.*
> *Understanding will keep you, to deliver*
> *you from the way of evil, from the men*
> *who speak perverse things;"* (PRO 2:10–12)

Wisdom is not only for the head. We have intellectualized wisdom and knowledge as being just for the mind. This is particularly true of business and leadership. But just as we are more than only a mind, wisdom impacts our whole being, body soul and spirit.

Wisdom enters out heart where it drives our very being in our will, emotions and behaviors. Knowledge is not just for the mind either as it enters our soul, that deepest essence of who we are.

The fruit of wisdom is, according to this scripture, discretion, and understanding. These great attributes, borne of wisdom will watch over us, keep us and deliver us. Not a bad set of outcomes for any leader to possess.

> **QUICK PRAYER:** Thank you for wisdom Lord,
> cause it to bear fruit in my life. Amen.

CHAPTER 3

My son, don't forget my teaching;
but let your heart keep my commandments:
for length of days, and years of life,
and peace, will they add to you.
Don't let kindness and truth forsake you.
Bind them around your neck.
Write them on the tablet of your heart.
So you will find favor,
and good understanding in the sight of God and man.
Trust in the LORD with all your heart,
and don't lean on your own understanding.
In all your ways acknowledge him,
and he will make your paths straight.
Don't be wise in your own eyes.
Fear the LORD, and depart from evil.
It will be health to your body,
and nourishment to your bones.
Honor the LORD with your substance,
with the first fruits of all your increase:
so your barns will be filled with plenty,
and your vats will overflow with new wine.
My son, don't despise the LORD's discipline,
neither be weary of his reproof:
for whom the LORD loves, he reproves;
even as a father reproves the son in whom he delights.

Happy is the man who finds wisdom,
the man who gets understanding.

SIX

MAKE SENSE

"Trust in the LORD with all your heart, and don't lean on your own understanding." (PRO 3:5)

How often do we take circumstances and try to figure out the meaning. We look at our business or things that happen and can't make sense of them. The pace of business and the marketplace is intense, we live in the midst of a digital revolution. The very way we transact and companies' function is being dislocated. When there is change there is always some chaos, and things happen we just don't understand.

An infinite God has a different perspective. How do we ever expect to understand him? We won't. His ways are not our ways, his thoughts not our thoughts. Sometimes we need to understand that we won't understand and just...trust.

Often just as we think we have God in a box, and understand Him, things change and the mystery continues. It is just a part of our walk with God. Why don't we just let God be God, we don't always have to understand.

QUICK PRAYER: I will trust You. Amen.

For her good profit is better than getting silver,

and her return is better than fine gold.

She is more precious than rubies.

None of the things you can desire are to be compared to her.

Length of days is in her right hand.

In her left hand are riches and honor.

Her ways are ways of pleasantness.

All her paths are peace.

She is a tree of life to those who lay hold of her.

Happy is everyone who retains her.

By wisdom the LORD founded the earth.

By understanding, he established the heavens.

By his knowledge, the depths were broken up,

and the skies drop down the dew.

My son, let them not depart from your eyes.

Keep sound wisdom and discretion:

so they will be life to your soul,

and grace for your neck.

Then you shall walk in your way securely.

Your foot won't stumble.

When you lie down, you will not be afraid.

Yes, you will lie down, and your sleep will be sweet.

Don't be afraid of sudden fear,

neither of the desolation of the wicked, when it comes:

for the LORD will be your confidence,

and will keep your foot from being taken.

SEVEN

FIRST

"Honor The LORD with your substance,
with the first fruits of all your increase:"
(PRO 3:9)

The principle of giving a portion is infused in the Scriptures. Honoring God with a holy portion, tithe, or sacrifice is a spiritual principle. If it is all His, why not honor Him with acknowledging His Lordship by bringing the tithe into the storehouse?

This is not a legalistic practice but a Godly discipline and acknowledgment that all we have comes from Him. It helps keep it all in perspective. We think so much about these things that a fresh perspective is probably not a bad thing.

The chances are as a leader you will be in the category of having enough supply to give away. Guarding our heart to ensure God has priority involves some discipline, planning and focus.

He doesn't need your money, but He does require your obedience. I have found that a surrendered heart moderates greed. Perhaps we need to give to receive.

> **QUICK PRAYER:** I will give You the best part of all You have given me, for You are my Lord. Amen.

Don't withhold good from those to whom it is due,

when it is in the power of your hand to do it.

Don't say to your neighbor, "Go, and come again;

tomorrow I will give it to you,"

when you have it by you.

Don't devise evil against your neighbor,

since he dwells securely by you.

Don't strive with a man without cause,

if he has done you no harm.

Don't envy the man of violence.

Choose none of his ways.

For the perverse is an abomination to the LORD,

but his friendship is with the upright.

the LORD's curse is in the house of the wicked,

but he blesses the habitation of the righteous.

Surely he mocks the mockers,

but he gives grace to the humble.

The wise will inherit glory,

but shame will be the promotion of fools.

EIGHT

PROMPT PAYMENT

"Don't say to your neighbor, "Go, and come again; tomorrow I will give it to you," when you have it by you." (PRO 3:28)

I like this description because it demonstrates the heart of God. There is something very right and proper about spontaneously meeting a need. If we have something in hand that can meet a need of others, we shouldn't even hesitate to give.

There is something inherently wrong with having resources and not meeting the need. Even in business, in the brutal cut and thrust of the commercial world, the principles of generosity apply.

We rely on suppliers to be able to do what we do, they are an intrinsic part of our own performance. Honouring them is in part reflected by how and when we pay them what is due.

If we can pay bills now, why not pay them now? This could cut across the prevailing culture and demonstrate a transformed life. Isn't that what we are supposed to be doing?

QUICK PRAYER: Help me to be prompt in my payments. Amen.

CHAPTER 4

Listen, sons, to a father's instruction.
Pay attention and know understanding;
for I give you sound learning.
Don't forsake my law.
For I was a son to my father,
tender and an only child in the sight of my mother.
He taught me, and said to me:
"Let your heart retain my words.
Keep my commandments, and live.
Get wisdom.
Get understanding.
Don't forget, neither swerve from the words of my mouth.
Don't forsake her, and she will preserve you.
Love her, and she will keep you.
Wisdom is supreme.
Get wisdom.
Yes, though it costs all your possessions, get understanding.
Esteem her, and she will exalt you.
She will bring you to honor, when you embrace her.
She will give to your head a garland of grace.
She will deliver a crown of splendor to you."

Listen, my son, and receive my sayings.
The years of your life will be many.
I have taught you in the way of wisdom.
I have led you in straight paths.
When you go, your steps will not be hampered.
When you run, you will not stumble.

NINE

WISDOM

"Don't forsake her, and she will preserve you.
Love her, and she will keep you." (PRO 4:6)

There are two kinds of wisdom: worldly wisdom and Godly wisdom. The worldly kind is fine, but in Godly wisdom we gain an eternal perspective and the wisdom of ages—the wisdom of a Creator who knows us intimately and formed us individually.

Pressing into God and seeking His wisdom has great benefit in all we do as we serve God in the marketplace. Godly wisdom is often in contrast to worldly wisdom, and the truly wise can discern the difference.

We live and lead in the real world, but don't underestimate the practical application of Godly wisdom.

True wisdom always originates with Him Who is wisdom. He is not only the origin of all true wisdom; He is wisdom itself. Wisdom is a characteristic of who God is. When you seek wisdom, you are seeking Him.

> **QUICK PRAYER**: Help me to truly seek Godly wisdom, Lord. Amen.

Take firm hold of instruction.

Don't let her go.

Keep her, for she is your life.

Don't enter into the path of the wicked.

Don't walk in the way of evil men.

Avoid it, and don't pass by it.

Turn from it, and pass on.

For they don't sleep, unless they do evil.

Their sleep is taken away, unless they make someone fall.

For they eat the bread of wickedness,

and drink the wine of violence.

But the path of the righteous is like the dawning light,

that shines more and more until the perfect day.

The way of the wicked is like darkness.

They don't know what they stumble over.

My son, attend to my words.

Turn your ear to my sayings.

Let them not depart from your eyes.

Keep them in the midst of your heart.

For they are life to those who find them,

and health to their whole body.

Keep your heart with all diligence,

for out of it is the wellspring of life.

Put away from yourself a perverse mouth.

Put corrupt lips far from you.

Let your eyes look straight ahead.

Fix your gaze directly before you.

TEN

PROTECT YOURSELF

*"Keep your heart with all diligence, for out
of it is the wellspring of life"* (PRO 4:23)

Our hearts are hard to understand. They are the wellspring of emotion, feelings, motivators, and passions. We can damage our hearts by exposing them to the wrong influences, and they can be deceptive.

Whilst the emotionless leader is an anathema to a servant hearted leader, we should have wisdom to ensure we engage emotionally in an appropriate way.

This Scripture tells us that everything we do flows from our hearts. Wow, now that is something we just do not understand. Even what we say is influenced as "out of our hearts our mouths speak" (Mat 12:34).

Be careful of potentially destructive relationships in your business and private world, and do your utmost to protect your heart. It is obviously an important part to protect.

> **QUICK PRAYER**: Help me guard my heart, Jesus.
> Amen.

Make the path of your feet level.

Let all of your ways be established.

Don't turn to the right hand nor to the left.

Remove your foot from evil.

CHAPTER 5

My son, pay attention to my wisdom.

Turn your ear to my understanding:

that you may maintain discretion,

that your lips may preserve knowledge.

For the lips of an adulteress drip honey.

Her mouth is smoother than oil,

But in the end she is as bitter as wormwood,

and as sharp as a two-edged sword.

Her feet go down to death.

Her steps lead straight to Sheol.

She gives no thought to the way of life.

Her ways are crooked, and she doesn't know it.

Now therefore, my sons, listen to me.

Don't depart from the words of my mouth.

Remove your way far from her.

Don't come near the door of her house,

lest you give your honor to others,

and your years to the cruel one;

lest strangers feast on your wealth,

and your labors enrich another man's house.

You will groan at your latter end,

when your flesh and your body are consumed,

and say, "How I have hated instruction,

and my heart despised reproof;

neither have I obeyed the voice of my teachers,

nor turned my ear to those who instructed me!

I have come to the brink of utter ruin,

in the midst of the gathered assembly."

ELEVEN

NEED DIRECTION

"She gives no thought to the way of life. Her ways are crooked, and she doesn't know it."
(PRO 5:6)

Where are you going? What are you trying to achieve? What is the future state of your company that you are aiming to get to? We all need direction in order to focus, to allocate resources, and to create vision and momentum. If we don't know where we are going, how will we know when we get there?

Don't be aimless and wander. Ask God for clarity of direction. He has a plan and purpose for your life, and your business. Part of our destiny is orchestrated and for part we need to partner with God, hear from Him, and impact our circumstances with faith prayer and action.

How can we be obedient if we do not hear, and how can we hear if we do not listen? Taking the time to offer commercial situations to God will yield a fruitful and successful outcome.

QUICK PRAYER: Show me Your way, Lord, that I may walk in it. Amen.

Drink water out of your own cistern,

running water out of your own well.

Should your springs overflow in the streets,

streams of water in the public squares?

Let them be for yourself alone,

not for strangers with you.

Let your spring be blessed.

Rejoice in the wife of your youth.

A loving doe and a graceful deer—

let her breasts satisfy you at all times.

Be captivated always with her love.

For why should you, my son, be captivated with an adulteress?

Why embrace the bosom of another?

For the ways of man are before the eyes of the LORD.

He examines all his paths.

The evil deeds of the wicked ensnare him.

The cords of his sin hold him firmly.

He will die for lack of instruction.

In the greatness of his folly, he will go astray.

TWELVE

STAY FAITHFUL

"Let your spring be blessed. Rejoice in the wife of your youth. A loving doe and a graceful deer— let her breasts satisfy you at all times. Be captivated always with her love." (PRO 5:18-19)

Isn't this meant to be a book about leadership? It is, and so is this scripture. God has a lot to say about the dangers of adultery in the 'Book of Proverbs'. As leaders we are not only not immune, but are often more vulnerable to the temptation. God doesn't mince His words, He made us and knows us well.

Long hours, business trips, family stress, working with teams, and other leadership challenges, can all make us susceptible to falling in this most ancient of ways.

Maintaining a strong close relationship with our wife or husband is absolutely paramount to successful leadership. Our personal relationship with our life p[partner has to take priority for us to be effective, both in the short and long term.

Not only do we need to commit time to this priority but also protect the relationship with great big firm boundaries and protection mechanisms. Being aware of the risk and the need to maintain purity in this area is vital. I've seen too many great people fall at this hurdle. Protect yourself, your partner and your leadership.

QUICK PRAYER: Let me always be captivated by my Partner. Amen.

CHAPTER 6

My **son, if you have become collateral for your neighbor,**
if you have struck your hands in pledge for a stranger;
You are trapped by the words of your mouth.
You are ensnared with the words of your mouth.
Do this now, my son, and deliver yourself,
since you have come into the hand of your neighbor.
Go, humble yourself.
Press your plea with your neighbor.
Give no sleep to your eyes,
nor slumber to your eyelids.
Free yourself, like a gazelle from the hand of the hunter,
like a bird from the snare of the fowler.

Go to the ant, you sluggard.
Consider her ways, and be wise;
which having no chief, overseer, or ruler,
provides her bread in the summer,
and gathers her food in the harvest.
How long will you sleep, sluggard?
When will you arise out of your sleep?
A little sleep, a little slumber,
a little folding of the hands to sleep:
so your poverty will come as a robber,
and your scarcity as an armed man.

A worthless person, a man of iniquity,
is he who walks with a perverse mouth;
who winks with his eyes, who signals with his feet,
who motions with his fingers;

THIRTEEN

RENEGOTIATE

> *"My son, if you have become collateral for your neighbor, if you have struck your hands in pledge for a stranger; You are trapped by the words of your mouth. You are ensnared with the words of your mouth."* (PRO 6:1–2)

The essence of this proverb occurs a number of times in Scripture. It's obviously an important financial principle, particularly for those of us who are in business.

If we are in onerous contracts or agreements or have guaranteed another entity or person, we need to renegotiate. Don't put off, don't delay, and don't get distracted or be put off by the inconvenience or how it may be perceived; go and get it changed.

The Bible describes it as a trap, that we have been ensnared by the words of our mouth. If it is God's will that we not enter into such an agreement, He will give us a way of escape.

He is faithful and will give you a way of escape. As we are obedient to His word He frees us, and ensures we are not ensnared by the enemy's plans.

QUICK PRAYER: Give me favor to renegotiate where I need to please, Lord. Amen.

in whose heart is perverseness,
who devises evil continually,
who always sows discord.
Therefore his calamity will come suddenly.
He will be broken suddenly, and that without remedy.

There are six things which the LORD hates;
yes, seven which are an abomination to him:
haughty eyes, a lying tongue,
hands that shed innocent blood;
a heart that devises wicked schemes,
feet that are swift in running to mischief,
a false witness who utters lies,
and he who sows discord among brothers.

My son, keep your father's commandment,
and don't forsake your mother's teaching.
Bind them continually on your heart.
Tie them around your neck.
When you walk, it will lead you.
When you sleep, it will watch over you.
When you awake, it will talk with you.
For the commandment is a lamp,
and the law is light.
Reproofs of instruction are the way of life,
to keep you from the immoral woman,
from the flattery of the wayward wife's tongue.
Don't lust after her beauty in your heart,
neither let her captivate you with her eyelids.

FOURTEEN

ANTS

*"Go to the ant, you sluggard. Consider her
ways and be wise;"* (PRO 6:6)

I don't like ants, they can be quite a nuisance; but they have enormous energy and strength. They never seem to rest. They are always productive and busy. There is a lesson of a need for application and hard work.

There is fruit from good, honest labor, focus, and application. If we wait for it to happen by itself, it probably won't. We have a responsibility to be productive with the gifts and resources given to us. In a very real way, we are, and will be, held accountable.

There is opportunity in leadership to ease up and get others to do all the hard work. Whilst delegation is an essential skill and empowerment releases potential, it does not obfuscate the need for our own application.

Take a moment to reflect on your work load. Are you focused and applying your resources with wisdom?

> **QUICK PRAYER**: Give me the focus and energy to
> be productive, Lord. Amen.

For a prostitute reduces you to a piece of bread.

The adulteress hunts for your precious life.

Can a man scoop fire into his lap,

and his clothes not be burned?

Or can one walk on hot coals,

and his feet not be scorched?

So is he who goes in to his neighbor's wife.

Whoever touches her will not be unpunished.

Men don't despise a thief,

if he steals to satisfy himself when he is hungry:

but if he is found, he shall restore seven times.

He shall give all the wealth of his house.

He who commits adultery with a woman is void of understanding.

He who does it destroys his own soul.

He will get wounds and dishonor.

His reproach will not be wiped away.

For jealousy arouses the fury of the husband.

He won't spare in the day of vengeance.

He won't regard any ransom,

neither will he rest content, though you give many gifts.

FIFTEEN

PLENTY

"Provides her bread in the summer, and gathers her food in the harvest." (PRO 6:8)

Life comes in seasons. There is a time to plant, a time to wait, a time to harvest, and a time to store away grain. How we act and what we do with our resources should be driven by an awareness of what season we are in. Economies have seasons, as do businesses.

Understanding the season your company, workplace or team are in, is essential as your strategy will need to be different depending on what the future holds.

Do not assume plenty will always be there. Alternatively, if you see no fruit but have sown faithfully, your harvest will be coming. Sometimes it rains in summer and the sun shines in winter. Discerning timing is a key part of a successful business. God can give you that insight.

QUICK PRAYER: Help me to be aware of what season I am in. Amen.

CHAPTER 7

My son, keep my words.
Lay up my commandments within you.
Keep my commandments and live!
Guard my teaching as the apple of your eye.
Bind them on your fingers.
Write them on the tablet of your heart.
Tell wisdom, "You are my sister."
Call understanding your relative,
that they may keep you from the strange woman,
from the foreigner who flatters with her words.
For at the window of my house,
I looked out through my lattice.
I saw among the simple ones.
I discerned among the youths a young man void of understanding,
passing through the street near her corner,
he went the way to her house,
in the twilight, in the evening of the day,
in the middle of the night and in the darkness.
Behold, there a woman met him with the attire of a prostitute,
and with crafty intent.
She is loud and defiant.
Her feet don't stay in her house.
Now she is in the streets, now in the squares,
and lurking at every corner.
So she caught him, and kissed him.
With an impudent face she said to him:
"Sacrifices of peace offerings are with me.
This day I have paid my vows.

SIXTEEN

RELATIVE WISDOM

"Bind them on your fingers. Write them on the tablet of your heart. Tell wisdom, "You are my sister." Call understanding your relative," (PRO 7: 4-5)

How important is it in God's view to seek after His wisdom. Maybe it is just one of those things we can occasionally indulge in when we think we need to. His description in this Proverb is quiet contrary to that view. In fact it is rendered so intimately that it sounds like hyperbole.

We are to take these words of wisdom and bind them to our fingers. That talks to me about the need to have them physically close, able to be drawn on immediately and a 'hands on' practical outworking of Godly wisdom.

We are to write them on our hearts. Mediate on His Word until it becomes a part of who we are. The assimilation process of God's word is often borne of intent, meditation and repetition.

Calling Wisdom and Understanding your closest relatives seems a bit odd but we are to be intimately associated with these characteristics and give them honor and high standing in our priorities. As we give time and place to God's Word and Wisdom it's fruit will manifest in our lives.

QUICK PRAYER: I honour wisdom Lord and will write it on my heart. Amen.

Therefore I came out to meet you,

to diligently seek your face,

and I have found you.

I have spread my couch with carpets of tapestry,

with striped cloths of the yarn of Egypt.

I have perfumed my bed with myrrh, aloes, and cinnamon.

Come, let's take our fill of loving until the morning.

Let's solace ourselves with loving.

For my husband isn't at home.

He has gone on a long journey.

He has taken a bag of money with him.

He will come home at the full moon."

With persuasive words, she led him astray.

With the flattering of her lips, she seduced him.

He followed her immediately,

as an ox goes to the slaughter,

as a fool stepping into a noose.

Until an arrow strikes through his liver,

as a bird hurries to the snare,

and doesn't know that it will cost his life.

Now therefore, sons, listen to me.

Pay attention to the words of my mouth.

Don't let your heart turn to her ways.

Don't go astray in her paths,

for she has thrown down many wounded.

Yes, all her slain are a mighty army.

Her house is the way to Sheol,

going down to the rooms of death.

SEVENTEEN

FLATTERY

> *"With persuasive words, she led him astray.*
> *With the flattering of her lips, she seduced him.*
> *He followed her immediately, as an ox goes to*
> *the slaughter, as a fool stepping into a noose.*
> (PRO 7: 21-22)

We all like to be admired. Leadership does attract attention from those in subordinate roles and from a larger section of community. It is easy to begin to believe that we are somehow special outside of our place in Christ.

Our vocation is just that, a calling of God aligned with the gifts and talents He has given us. All we have and all we are is from Him. When we are not fully centered in that reality we can succumb to the flattery of others and get puffed up with pride.

A vulnerably to flattery, that we all have to some measure, makes us vulnerable to exploitation and manipulation. The price of which can be quite devastating. In this instance a fall into adultery and its dire consequence.

But the principal is just as relevant in business. If you are being flattered, it maybe a genuine compliment or it may be, as it often is, the desire of the other party to ingratiate themselves, based on some other agenda.

QUICK PRAYER: Protect me from flattering lips Lord, my self esteem is in You. Amen.

CHAPTER 8

Doesn't wisdom cry out?
Doesn't understanding raise her voice?
On the top of high places by the way,
where the paths meet, she stands.
Beside the gates, at the entry of the city,
at the entry doors, she cries aloud:
"To you men, I call!
I send my voice to the sons of mankind.
You simple, understand prudence.
You fools, be of an understanding heart.
Hear, for I will speak excellent things.
The opening of my lips is for right things.
For my mouth speaks truth.
Wickedness is an abomination to my lips.
All the words of my mouth are in righteousness.
There is nothing crooked or perverse in them.
They are all plain to him who understands,
right to those who find knowledge.
Receive my instruction rather than silver;
knowledge rather than choice gold.
For wisdom is better than rubies.
All the things that may be desired can't be compared to it.

"I, wisdom, have made prudence my dwelling.
Find out knowledge and discretion.
The fear of the LORD is to hate evil.
I hate pride, arrogance, the evil way, and the perverse mouth.
Counsel and sound knowledge are mine.

EIGHTEEN

PRICELESS

"For wisdom is better than rubies. All the things that may be desired can't be compared to it." (PRO 8:11)

Imagine a great big pile of precious stones, diamonds, sapphires and rubies. A literal goldmine of wealth. What would we do to attain this wealth? We all work hard to build a better future and provide for our families, ourselves, and the wider community. We in business value profit and monetary reward, and there is nothing wrong with that.

What we don't do, at least I find I don't do, is value wisdom above rubies. It may be just me, but then again maybe not. God says quite clearly that His Wisdom is more valuable than rubies. Then He 'ups the ante' to say it is more valuable than anything that can be desired. Anything? Wait, could that be right?

If God who created us is saying His wisdom should be pursued and valued more than anything else, we all have some readjustment of our priorities required.

Often our time with Him or study of the Word is pushed into an available corner of time rather than made a priority. This Proverb would suggest, or insist, that it become an absolute imperative, as it is the foundation to all other worthwhile things.

QUICK PRAYER: Forgive me for not valuing Your wisdom as I should. Amen.

I have understanding and power.
By me kings reign,
and princes decree justice.
By me princes rule;
nobles, and all the righteous rulers of the earth.
I love those who love me.
Those who seek me diligently will find me.
With me are riches, honor,
enduring wealth, and prosperity.
My fruit is better than gold, yes, than fine gold;
my yield than choice silver.
I walk in the way of righteousness,
in the midst of the paths of justice;
That I may give wealth to those who love me.
I fill their treasuries.

"the LORD possessed me in the beginning of his work,
before his deeds of old.
I was set up from everlasting, from the beginning,
before the earth existed.
When there were no depths, I was brought forth,
when there were no springs abounding with water.
Before the mountains were settled in place,
before the hills, I was brought forth;
while as yet he had not made the earth, nor the fields,
nor the beginning of the dust of the world.
When he established the heavens, I was there;
when he set a circle on the surface of the deep,

NINETEEN

GOOD FRUIT

"With me are riches, honor, enduring wealth, and prosperity." (Pro 8:18)

Wow! The fruit of wisdom does look good to me. Who would not like some riches, honor, wealth and prosperity. But the Bible clearly says that those who pursue riches, wander from the faith and pierce themselves with many sorrows. Ecclesiastes also attributed to Solomon, says that God has given us the ability to create wealth and with it He adds no sorrow.

These seem to contradict each other and be diametrically opposed. The difference, as I perceive it is this; It depends on what you are pursuing.

If you are pursuing wealth and riches you will reap the downside consequences mentioned. If you are seeking God, His righteousness, His wisdom and His Kingdom the all these things will be added to you are well.

The outcome of seeking Him is the fruit of wisdom, they are a consequence of pursuing God and being obedient to Him. Seeking wealth for wealth's sake even dressed up in religiosity will ultimately bring consequences that are unwanted.

There is a price to pay. Only the righteous fruit of God's blessing, a consequence of His wisdom are given with no sorrow. It is a subtle and narrow difference with dramatic and diverse outcomes. Let's not fool ourselves with our true motivations.

QUICK PRAYER: Thank you for the fruit of wisdom, help me to keep my eyes on You. Amen.

when he established the clouds above,

when the springs of the deep became strong,

when he gave to the sea its boundary,

that the waters should not violate his commandment,

when he marked out the foundations of the earth;

then I was the craftsman by his side.

I was a delight day by day,

always rejoicing before him,

Rejoicing in his whole world.

My delight was with the sons of men.

"Now therefore, my sons, listen to me,

for blessed are those who keep my ways.

Hear instruction, and be wise.

Don't refuse it.

Blessed is the man who hears me,

watching daily at my gates,

waiting at my door posts.

For whoever finds me, finds life,

and will obtain favor from the LORD.

But he who sins against me wrongs his own soul.

All those who hate me love death."

CHAPTER 9

Wisdom has built her house.

She has carved out her seven pillars.

She has prepared her meat.

She has mixed her wine.

She has also set her table.

She has sent out her maidens.

She cries from the highest places of the city:

"Whoever is simple, let him turn in here!"

As for him who is void of understanding, she says to him,

"Come, eat some of my bread,

Drink some of the wine which I have mixed!

Leave your simple ways, and live.

Walk in the way of understanding."

He who corrects a mocker invites insult.

He who reproves a wicked man invites abuse.

Don't reprove a scoffer, lest he hate you.

Reprove a wise man, and he will love you.

Instruct a wise man, and he will be still wiser.

Teach a righteous man, and he will increase in learning.

The fear of the LORD is the beginning of wisdom.

The knowledge of the Holy One is understanding.

For by me your days will be multiplied.

The years of your life will be increased.

If you are wise, you are wise for yourself.

If you mock, you alone will bear it.

The foolish woman is loud,

Undisciplined, and knows nothing.

TWENTY

MOCKER

> *"He who corrects a mocker invites insult. He who reproves a wicked man invites abuse. Don't reprove a scoffer, lest he hate you. Reprove a wise man, and he will love you."* (PRO 9:7-8)

Leaders have an obligation to unlock and realize the potential of those under their authority. They do that through serving, guiding and encouraging, but also through challenging and stretching. Every so often we need to reprove, correct and bring discipline.

Sometimes as Christians we are reluctant to engage in this way. I think that is more as a result of an error in Christian culture rather than a true Biblical understanding. Being 'nice' is not Christian, if it is an abdication of our responsibility to confront, reprove and correct. Yes it must be done with Godly wisdom, and in a spirit of reconciliation and service to the individual involved. But done it must be.

Notice the reaction here is not related to the rebuke, but to the character of the recipient. Obviously that is assuming it is done in a wise and reasonable way, by someone fully aware of their own need for grace. The wise will respect and respond to the reproof, the mocker and scoffer will not. Sometimes discernment of character ahead of time will avoid unnecessary confrontation.

QUICK PRAYER: Help me to see who is wise and who is not, and give me the courage to correct when led by you. Amen.

She sits at the door of her house,

on a seat in the high places of the city,

To call to those who pass by,

who go straight on their ways,

"Whoever is simple, let him turn in here."

as for him who is void of understanding, she says to him,

"Stolen water is sweet.

Food eaten in secret is pleasant."

But he doesn't know that the dead are there,

that her guests are in the depths of Sheol.

TWENTY ONE

UNDERSTANDING

"The fear of the LORD is the beginning of wisdom. The knowledge of the Holy One is understanding." (PRO 9:10)

I don't know about you, but I could do with more understanding—in particular an understanding that comes from the revelation of listening to the Holy Spirit. He is waiting to be invited into your business and wants to walk with you, guiding, leading, empowering, and bringing understanding.

God is our greatest resource, He is for us and not against us, He has plans for us and our places of work, He is vitally interested in our everyday work. It is what He has called us to.

Let's not relegate God's wisdom and our understanding to a seemingly sacred context. Being vitally interested in our vocation, our calling at work, He is always willing to give insight. Invite Him into your business world again today.

> **QUICK PRAYER**: Help me to walk closely with You, Holy Spirit. Amen.

CHAPTER 10

The proverbs of Solomon.

A wise son makes a glad father;
but a foolish son brings grief to his mother.

Treasures of wickedness profit nothing,

but righteousness delivers from death.

the LORD will not allow the soul of the righteous to go hungry,

but he thrusts away the desire of the wicked.

He becomes poor who works with a lazy hand,

but the hand of the diligent brings wealth.

He who gathers in summer is a wise son,

but he who sleeps during the harvest is a son who causes shame.

Blessings are on the head of the righteous,

but violence covers the mouth of the wicked.

The memory of the righteous is blessed,

but the name of the wicked will rot.

The wise in heart accept commandments,

but a chattering fool will fall.

He who walks blamelessly walks surely,

but he who perverts his ways will be found out.

One winking with the eye causes sorrow,

but a chattering fool will fall.

The mouth of the righteous is a spring of life,

but violence covers the mouth of the wicked.

Hatred stirs up strife,

but love covers all wrongs.

Wisdom is found on the lips of him who has discernment,

but a rod is for the back of him who is void of understanding.

TWENTY TWO

DILIGENCE

"He becomes poor who works with a lazy hand, but the hand of the diligent brings wealth." (PRO 10:4)

We are often quick to blame God for all our problems. Other people and circumstances are reasonable targets as well. It is always easier to look elsewhere when blame is to be apportioned.

This is not about a guilt trip, and I certainly wouldn't want to place any condemnation on you, but when we do not apply ourselves to the tasks assigned to us, there are consequences that are real and physical, including missing a promotion or being disciplined at work.

If we are the leader we need to take responsibility for the team's outcomes and performance. Culture comes from the top and we set the tone for the team.

The Bible says lazy hands lead to poverty, yet the hope is that He is always ready to help you with a turnaround. The outcome He wants is for you to be blessed, and diligent hands bring wealth.

> **QUICK PRAYER**: I'm sorry for when I slack off.
> Help me to work well and wisely. Amen.

Wise men lay up knowledge,

but the mouth of the foolish is near ruin.

The rich man's wealth is his strong city.

The destruction of the poor is their poverty.

The labor of the righteous leads to life.

The increase of the wicked leads to sin.

He is in the way of life who heeds correction,

but he who forsakes reproof leads others astray.

He who hides hatred has lying lips.

He who utters a slander is a fool.

In the multitude of words there is no lack of disobedience,

but he who restrains his lips does wisely.

The tongue of the righteous is like choice silver.

The heart of the wicked is of little worth.

The lips of the righteous feed many,

but the foolish die for lack of understanding.

the LORD's blessing brings wealth,

and he adds no trouble to it.

It is a fool's pleasure to do wickedness,

but wisdom is a man of understanding's pleasure.

What the wicked fear, will overtake them,

but the desire of the righteous will be granted.

When the whirlwind passes, the wicked is no more;

but the righteous stand firm forever.

As vinegar to the teeth, and as smoke to the eyes,

so is the sluggard to those who send him.

The fear of the LORD prolongs days,

but the years of the wicked shall be shortened.

TWENTY THREE

HARVEST

"He who gathers in summer is a wise son,
but he who sleeps during the harvest is a son
who causes shame." (PRO 10:5)

There is wisdom in understanding the season you are in. There is a time to reap and a time to sow; other times are winter, where nothing seems to happen and patience is required.

The responsibility we have in summer is to reap the harvest. We can be in different seasons in different areas of our lives at the same time. Discerning what season we are in is important. There is no point in sowing in winter.

There are financial harvests, spiritual harvests, and even relationship harvests. What season are you in now, and what area is ready for harvest? We have to be diligent and aware, for the season of harvest is short and temporary.

Discerning the season for our commercial enterprise of team is part of our leadership responsibilities, particularly when it is time to harvest.

> **QUICK PRAYER**: Help me to bring in the harvest. I commit to bringing it all in and using it wisely. Amen.

The prospect of the righteous is joy,

but the hope of the wicked will perish.

The way of the LORD is a stronghold to the upright,

but it is a destruction to the workers of iniquity.

The righteous will never be removed,

but the wicked will not dwell in the land.

The mouth of the righteous brings forth wisdom,

but the perverse tongue will be cut off.

The lips of the righteous know what is acceptable,

but the mouth of the wicked is perverse.

TWENTY FOUR

FOUNTAIN

> *"The mouth of the righteous is a spring of*
> *life, but violence covers the mouth of the*
> *wicked."* (PRO 10:11)

Fountains are wonderful. They are refreshing, life giving, beautiful, and awe-inspiring. Our words should refresh, encourage, and inspire those around us.

The alternative doesn't bear too much consideration. Today be aware of what you say. Are you speaking life or death? Your mouth should be a fountain of life.

Try and be conscious of what you say and its possible impact. If you are anything like me, you will be surprised by how little you say that enlightens the life of others. Maybe that is why the wise seem to speak little and listen a lot.

God has given us responsibly as leaders to grow, nourish and encourage those whom he has entrusted to us. It is a responsibility we should not take lightly, particularly in how and what we say.

Look for the opportunity to refresh someone at work this week. You well may be surprised by the reaction, though I would hope it is not one of total surprise.

> **QUICK PRAYER**: Let the words of my mouth
> refresh others. Amen.

CHAPTER 11

A false balance is an abomination to the LORD,
but accurate weights are his delight.

When pride comes, then comes shame,
but with humility comes wisdom.

The integrity of the upright shall guide them,
but the perverseness of the treacherous shall destroy them.

Riches don't profit in the day of wrath,
but righteousness delivers from death.

The righteousness of the blameless will direct his way,
but the wicked shall fall by his own wickedness.

The righteousness of the upright shall deliver them,
but the unfaithful will be trapped by evil desires.

When a wicked man dies, hope perishes,
and expectation of power comes to nothing.

A righteous person is delivered out of trouble,
and the wicked takes his place.

With his mouth the godless man destroys his neighbor,
but the righteous will be delivered through knowledge.

When it goes well with the righteous, the city rejoices.
When the wicked perish, there is shouting.

By the blessing of the upright, the city is exalted,
but it is overthrown by the mouth of the wicked.

One who despises his neighbor is void of wisdom,
but a man of understanding holds his peace.

One who brings gossip betrays a confidence,
but one who is of a trustworthy spirit is one who keeps a secret.

Where there is no wise guidance, the nation falls,
but in the multitude of counselors there is victory.

TWENTY FIVE

TONGUE HOLDING

"One who despises his neighbor is void of wisdom, but a man of understanding holds his peace." (PRO 11:12)

Sometimes the best thing you can say is nothing at all. Giving someone a piece of your mind may be a piece you can ill afford to lose.

There is grace in overlooking an offense, mercy in not taking retribution, and forgiveness in answering gently to a harsh critic. Grace, mercy, and forgiveness are all things that have been freely given to us.

Leaders sometimes seem to act with impunity and 'cut loose' on staff when things don't go our way. There is no place for such behaviour in the workplace or in the Kingdom in any of its expression.

Let's treat others as God has treated us. Thank goodness He does not give us what we deserve. Why not treat others as God treats us? Our businesses will be all the better for it.

> **QUICK PRAYER:** Help me bite my tongue sometimes, please, Lord. Amen.

He who is collateral for a stranger will suffer for it,

but he who refuses pledges of collateral is secure.

A gracious woman obtains honor,

but violent men obtain riches.

The merciful man does good to his own soul,

but he who is cruel troubles his own flesh.

Wicked people earn deceitful wages,

but one who sows righteousness reaps a sure reward.

He who is truly righteous gets life.

He who pursues evil gets death.

Those who are perverse in heart are an abomination to the LORD,

but those whose ways are blameless are his delight.

Most certainly, the evil man will not be unpunished,

but the seed of the righteous will be delivered.

Like a gold ring in a pig's snout,

is a beautiful woman who lacks discretion.

The desire of the righteous is only good.

The expectation of the wicked is wrath.

There is one who scatters, and increases yet more.

There is one who withholds more than is appropriate, but gains poverty.

The liberal soul shall be made fat.

He who waters shall be watered also himself.

People curse someone who withholds grain,

but blessing will be on the head of him who sells it.

He who diligently seeks good seeks favor,

but he who searches after evil, it shall come to him.

He who trusts in his riches will fall,

TWENTY SIX

SECRETS

> *"One who brings gossip betrays a confidence,*
> *but one who is of a trustworthy spirit is one*
> *who keeps a secret."* (PRO 11:13)

Gossip is described in Scripture as a "choice morsel," and often it is. Perhaps it is a juicy bit of gossip only a few know. Or maybe we have been entrusted with a secret, a confidence has been entrusted to us. How do we respond?

This is an important question because our ability to keep a secret speaks to our character. Being a person of integrity with an ability to be trusted makes us a safe place. When we are trusted, what we say is listened to. It takes a lot to build trust and only a single event to destroy it.

Great culture is built on trust and trust on transparency. This can only be achieved in an atmosphere where your integrity is unquestioned, and our reputation sound.

Our reputations are intrinsically intertwined with the reputation of Him Whom we serve. When we let ourselves down, we tarnish God's reputation because we declare Him as our Lord.

QUICK PRAYER: Please help me to be trustworthy, Lord. Amen.

but the righteous shall flourish as the green leaf.

He who troubles his own house shall inherit the wind.

The foolish shall be servant to the wise of heart.

The fruit of the righteous is a tree of life.

He who is wise wins souls.

Behold, the righteous shall be repaid in the earth;

how much more the wicked and the sinner!

TWENTY SEVEN

KINGDOM LAW

> *"There is one who scatters, and increases yet more. There is one who withholds more than is appropriate, but gains poverty."* (PRO 11:24)

In the world, we are taught that if we are tight with our money, we will get more, yet the law of the kingdom is the opposite. Give and it will be given unto you. Withhold and you will come to poverty. It sounds upside down, but how often is that true with the things that God asks of us? He had to die to bring life. Death led to victory.

There is very often joy in obedience. As we give, it changes our hearts. Have you met a happy person who is stingy or a very generous person who is not happy? The Bible also tells us that it is God who gives us the gift of enjoying wealth. I think this comes from having a generous heart.

This is as applicable in a commercial environment as it is in our personal lives. Companies and leaders who understand this dynamic build companies that prosper.

QUICK PRAYER: Holy Spirit, please cause me to have a generous heart, a fruit of Your presence in me. Amen.

CHAPTER 12

Whoever loves correction loves knowledge,
but he who hates reproof is stupid.

A good man shall obtain favor from the LORD,
but he will condemn a man of wicked devices.

A man shall not be established by wickedness,
but the root of the righteous shall not be moved.

A worthy woman is the crown of her husband,
but a disgraceful wife is as rottenness in his bones.

The thoughts of the righteous are just,
but the advice of the wicked is deceitful.

The words of the wicked are about lying in wait for blood,
but the speech of the upright rescues them.

The wicked are overthrown, and are no more,
but the house of the righteous shall stand.

A man shall be commended according to his wisdom,
but he who has a warped mind shall be despised.

Better is he who is lightly esteemed, and has a servant,
than he who honors himself, and lacks bread.

A righteous man respects the life of his animal,
but the tender mercies of the wicked are cruel.

He who tills his land shall have plenty of bread,
but he who chases fantasies is void of understanding.

The wicked desires the plunder of evil men,
but the root of the righteous flourishes.

An evil man is trapped by sinfulness of lips,
but the righteous shall come out of trouble.

A man shall be satisfied with good by the fruit of his mouth.
The work of a man's hands shall be rewarded to him.

TWENTY EIGHT

CORRECTION

> *"Whoever loves correction loves knowledge, but*
> *he who hates reproof is stupid."* (PRO 12:1)

It is easy to forget that God is our Father, and like all good fathers, He will bring correction and discipline from time to time. This is often manifested in difficult circumstances or a word from someone else. How should we react to these events?

Getting before God to understand what adjustments He wants to make in us is a good start. We can be thankful that we have a loving Father who wants the best for us. Our position in receiving discipline and correction will determine our ultimate altitude in life and our walk with Him.

Let us not believe our own press and see our worldly leadership role as some sort of abdication of our responsibility to continue to grow and hear from God.

If you keep getting a "Why am I here again?" feeling, you may not have learned the lesson yet.

QUICK PRAYER: I need Your correction in my life, Lord. Help me to be aware. Amen.

The way of a fool is right in his own eyes,

but he who is wise listens to counsel.

A fool shows his annoyance the same day,

but one who overlooks an insult is prudent.

He who is truthful testifies honestly,

but a false witness lies.

There is one who speaks rashly like the piercing of a sword,

but the tongue of the wise heals.

Truth's lips will be established forever,

but a lying tongue is only momentary.

Deceit is in the heart of those who plot evil,

but joy comes to the promoters of peace.

No mischief shall happen to the righteous,

but the wicked shall be filled with evil.

Lying lips are an abomination to the LORD,

but those who do the truth are his delight.

A prudent man keeps his knowledge,

but the hearts of fools proclaim foolishness.

The hands of the diligent ones shall rule,

but laziness ends in slave labor.

Anxiety in a man's heart weighs it down,

but a kind word makes it glad.

A righteous person is cautious in friendship,

but the way of the wicked leads them astray.

The slothful man doesn't roast his game,

but the possessions of diligent men are prized.

In the way of righteousness is life;

in its path there is no death.

TWENTY NINE

RESULTS

"He who tills his land shall have plenty of bread, but he who chases fantasies is void of understanding." (PRO 12:11)

There is always something enticing about the latest idea, the new venture that is still shiny in its new box. We can spend a lot of time on the new when the slightly old has lost its shine.

There is enough entrepreneur in each of us to see many possibilities, but often we need to land the ones we have, before taking on more. It can be very frustrating for teams when the focus and agreed direction is lost in the excitement of a leader's new idea.

There is a time to explore new opportunities, and there is a time for good, old-fashioned, hard graft where we knuckle down and work hard on what we already have.

In its extreme, the entrepreneurial spirit can be distracted by the next idea while the last one dies on the shelf for lack of focus and resources. Sometimes we need to complete the last venture and not start a new thing.

> **QUICK PRAYER:** Keep me focused on the task at hand please, Holy Spirit. Amen.

THIRTY

LIP FRUIT

> *"A man shall be satisfied with good by the fruit of his mouth. The work of a man's hands shall be rewarded to him."* (PRO 12:14)

Do you want to be filled with good things? Speak well and work hard. These two things go hand in hand. Individually they have an effect and together they produce good fruit. God says that as you operate in this way, you will be filled with good things and rewarded.

In business and our personal lives, we impact people. What we say has the power to build up or tear down. That influence on people often determines our success in all realms of life.

We can say good things and do good things. Both are important and part of our witness at work. As leaders we set the tone and our teams are a reflection of us. How we treat others, what we say and how we say it, will be echoed across our organisations.

QUICK PRAYER: Thank You that You value good words and good work. Amen.

CHAPTER 13

A wise son listens to his father's instruction,
but a scoffer doesn't listen to rebuke.

By the fruit of his lips, a man enjoys good things;

but the unfaithful crave violence.

He who guards his mouth guards his soul.

One who opens wide his lips comes to ruin.

The soul of the sluggard desires, and has nothing,

but the desire of the diligent shall be fully satisfied.

A righteous man hates lies,

but a wicked man brings shame and disgrace.

Righteousness guards the way of integrity,

but wickedness overthrows the sinner.

There are some who pretend to be rich, yet have nothing.

There are some who pretend to be poor, yet have great wealth.

The ransom of a man's life is his riches,

but the poor hear no threats.

The light of the righteous shines brightly,

but the lamp of the wicked is snuffed out.

Pride only breeds quarrels,

but with ones who take advice is wisdom.

Wealth gained dishonestly dwindles away,

but he who gathers by hand makes it grow.

Hope deferred makes the heart sick,

but when longing is fulfilled, it is a tree of life.

Whoever despises instruction will pay for it,

but he who respects a command will be rewarded.

The teaching of the wise is a spring of life,

to turn from the snares of death.

THIRTY ONE

HATE

"A righteous man hates lies, but a wicked man brings shame and disgrace." (PRO 13:5)

Hate sounds like such a negative emotion and largely that is true. Yet we are called to have a heart after God.

He experiences hate and anger and a righteous indignation, and so should we. It is Ok to hate what is false, to get angry about injustice and sin and the work of the enemy. We are encouraged to be angry yet not sin.

As leaders, our walk with God in the workplace doesn't mean we become automatons, devoid of any emotion. We still are who we are. Sometimes we are frightened of our own emotive responses, as if they were purely fleshly and somewhat base.

Yet Jesus wept, tossed people out of the temple, and often had a strong word to say to the religious that I am sure wasn't delivered in a dovelike monotone. He is our model of leadership and one that turned the world upside down.

QUICK PRAYER: I hate what You hate, Lord. Amen.

Good understanding wins favor;

but the way of the unfaithful is hard.

Every prudent man acts from knowledge,

but a fool exposes folly.

A wicked messenger falls into trouble,

but a trustworthy envoy gains healing.

Poverty and shame come to him who refuses discipline,

but he who heeds correction shall be honored.

Longing fulfilled is sweet to the soul,

but fools detest turning from evil.

One who walks with wise men grows wise,

but a companion of fools suffers harm.

Misfortune pursues sinners,

but prosperity rewards the righteous.

A good man leaves an inheritance to his children's children,

but the wealth of the sinner is stored for the righteous.

An abundance of food is in poor people's fields,

but injustice sweeps it away.

One who spares the rod hates his son,

but one who loves him is careful to discipline him.

The righteous one eats to the satisfying of his soul,

but the belly of the wicked goes hungry.

THIRTY TWO

LITTLE

> *"Wealth gained dishonestly dwindles away,*
> *but he who gathers by hand makes it grow"*
> (PRO 13:11)

Those get rich quick schemes draw people in because the desire to get wealth outweighs their common sense of testing an opportunity. The old saying is that if it looks too good to be true, then it probably is.

Our strategies at work need to take this into account to be effective in pursuing opportunity whilst avoiding pitfalls. Our gains need to be based on a firm foundation in order to be truly fruitful and sustainable.

If we take shortcuts in how we earn, whether that is in overcharging, having an inferior product, dodging taxes, or not paying our creditors, God will not honor our income. It becomes fleeting and fragile, built on an unsure foundation.

When we do it right, earn an honest income, and invest wisely, it may seem to be little by little, but you will build a solid foundation that God will look at and cause to grow.

QUICK PRAYER: Keep me away from the quick fix and illusion of fast money. Amen.

THIRTY THREE

WISE COMPANY

"One who walks with wise men grows wise,
but a companion of fools suffers harm."
(PRO 13:20)

The people we spend time with will impact our lives. They will either be impacted for good, or they'll be impacted the bad. How would you rate the people you mix with? That sounds like a very harsh judgment or question. And yes, we are called to mix with those who need to know Jesus. There is nothing wrong with this; in fact, there is a lot of good in mixing with those who have yet to come to know Him.

Yet those who are close to us and those we choose to seek advice from will impact our lives. If we want to be wise, it would be prudent to walk with the wise. Be careful to choose the company you keep wisely.

It is as important in the places we work and who we work for as well as our own teams. Those we seek counsel from, and who we are friends of, will influence who we become, its as simple as that.

> **QUICK PRAYER**: Open my eyes to the wise around me. Amen.

CHAPTER 14

Every wise woman builds her house,
but the foolish one tears it down with her own hands.

He who walks in his uprightness fears the LORD,

but he who is perverse in his ways despises him.

The fool's talk brings a rod to his back,

but the lips of the wise protect them.

Where no oxen are, the crib is clean,

but much increase is by the strength of the ox.

A truthful witness will not lie,

but a false witness pours out lies.

A scoffer seeks wisdom, and doesn't find it,

but knowledge comes easily to a discerning person.

Stay away from a foolish man,

for you won't find knowledge on his lips.

The wisdom of the prudent is to think about his way,

but the folly of fools is deceit.

Fools mock at making atonement for sins,

but among the upright there is good will.

The heart knows its own bitterness and joy;

he will not share these with a stranger.

The house of the wicked will be overthrown,

but the tent of the upright will flourish.

There is a way which seems right to a man,

but in the end it leads to death.

Even in laughter the heart may be sorrowful,

and mirth may end in heaviness.

The unfaithful will be repaid for his own ways;

likewise a good man will be rewarded for his ways.

THIRTY FOUR

CREATIVE CHAOS

> *"Where no oxen are, the crib is clean, but*
> *much increase is by the strength of the ox."*
> (PRO 14:4)

Some people like businesses that operate with mechanistic efficiency and autocratic fervor. Personally, I think they lack soul and personality. More importantly, some cultures will alienate the innovative and entrepreneurial spirit by being overly authoritarian and controlling.

I believe we need to have clear vision and common purpose, but empowerment is an important component of sustainable growth. When we release our people, we unlock their potential. That can have a multiplier effect and create huge momentum.

Does it bring some chaos and mess? Oh yes, definitely, but it also brings the success based on the unlocked potential of an empowered workforce.

QUICK PRAYER: Thank You for creative chaos.
Amen.

A simple man believes everything,

but the prudent man carefully considers his ways.

A wise man fears, and shuns evil,

but the fool is hotheaded and reckless.

He who is quick to become angry will commit folly,

and a crafty man is hated.

The simple inherit folly,

but the prudent are crowned with knowledge.

The evil bow down before the good,

and the wicked at the gates of the righteous.

The poor person is shunned even by his own neighbor,

but the rich person has many friends.

He who despises his neighbor sins,

but blessed is he who has pity on the poor.

Don't they go astray who plot evil?

But love and faithfulness belong to those who plan good.

In all hard work there is profit,

but the talk of the lips leads only to poverty.

The crown of the wise is their riches,

but the folly of fools crowns them with folly.

A truthful witness saves souls,

but a false witness is deceitful.

In the fear of the LORD is a secure fortress,

and he will be a refuge for his children.

The fear of the LORD is a fountain of life,

turning people from the snares of death.

In the multitude of people is the king's glory,

but in the lack of people is the destruction of the prince.

THIRTY FIVE

FORWARD

"There is a way which seems right to a man,
but in the end it leads to death." (PRO 14:12)

Sometimes our natural tendencies can come to the fore. Pausing to seek God's wisdom can often shift our view and may save us from an unseen consequence. It is worth considering that we are not always right and that God has a better view.

Make sure God is included in your plans, or more correctly make sure you are included in His. He will put desires in your heart that align with His will, but we need to be in close relationship with Him for that dynamic to work well. Often what we think is right may not be, listen and learn and be obedient to the still quiet voice of the Holy Spirit.

When we belong to God, we are in His kingdom, under His jurisdiction. To prosper in this realm, we need to follow the auspices of the King. Doing it God's way should be our prime modus operandi, even when it doesn't make worldly sense. But occasionally we need some specific insight. Asking God and expecting an answer is part and parcel of a walk with a personal Savior.

QUICK PRAYER: Show me Your way, Lord, that I may walk in it. Amen.

He who is slow to anger has great understanding,

but he who has a quick temper displays folly.

The life of the body is a heart at peace,

but envy rots the bones.

He who oppresses the poor shows contempt for his Maker,

but he who is kind to the needy honors him.

The wicked is brought down in his calamity,

but in death, the righteous has a refuge.

Wisdom rests in the heart of one who has understanding,

and is even made known in the inward part of fools.

Righteousness exalts a nation,

but sin is a disgrace to any people.

The king's favor is toward a servant who deals wisely,

but his wrath is toward one who causes shame.

THIRTY SIX

TALKER

"In all hard work there is profit, but the talk
of the lips leads only to poverty." (PRO 14:23)

I have plenty of things I am going to get around to. If I talk about them for years, they still won't get done. It is only when we stop talking and start doing that we make progress.

Our words have to translate into action to be effective. If you want to talk about the latest idea, project, business model, or whatever, put timeframes into the discussion. This can help you crystalize a plan and start to progress to action.

A plan has milestones and clear demonstrable outcomes. Don't just talk, write it down, tell someone and become accountable to clear objectives and firm deadlines.

It is a lot easier to talk than to work. It is the easier option. It is hard work that brings a profitable result. Talk without action leads only to more talk and no outcome.

> **QUICK PRAYER**: I will do what I say and
> prevaricate less. Amen.

CHAPTER 15

A gentle answer turns away wrath,
but a harsh word stirs up anger.
The tongue of the wise commends knowledge,
but the mouth of fools gush out folly.
the LORD's eyes are everywhere,
keeping watch on the evil and the good.
A gentle tongue is a tree of life,
but deceit in it crushes the spirit.
A fool despises his father's correction,
but he who heeds reproof shows prudence.
In the house of the righteous is much treasure,
but the income of the wicked brings trouble.
The lips of the wise spread knowledge;
not so with the heart of fools.
The sacrifice made by the wicked is an abomination to the LORD,
but the prayer of the upright is his delight.
The way of the wicked is an abomination to the LORD,
but he loves him who follows after righteousness.
There is stern discipline for one who forsakes the way:
whoever hates reproof shall die.
Sheol and Abaddon are before the LORD—
how much more then the hearts of the children of men!
A scoffer doesn't love to be reproved;
he will not go to the wise.
A glad heart makes a cheerful face;
but an aching heart breaks the spirit.
The heart of one who has understanding seeks knowledge,
but the mouths of fools feed on folly.

THIRTY SEVEN

BE GENTLE

"A gentle answer turns away wrath, but a harsh word stirs up anger." (PRO 15:1)

When we are in a position of authority in our company, there is a temptation to be harsh. We can easily display emotions that are not appropriate. This is especially true when we are faced with an angry person.

The wisdom of this Scripture is that an unexpectedly gentle response can disarm a potentially volatile situation. Often when we are challenged, we may assume a gentle answer is a sign of weakness and that authority demands a certain demeanor. This Scripture would indicate a better way.

Gentleness is not weakness, often it is an expression of an inner strength, a transformed heart, one full of the peace of God. Your gentle response is a witness.

Leadership does not demand that we act in a harsh or distant manner. Our example is Jesus. How did He act? Take a look in the gospels for an example of true leadership in action.

QUICK PRAYER: Help me to be gentle. Amen.

All the days of the afflicted are wretched,

but one who has a cheerful heart enjoys a continual feast.

Better is little, with the fear of the LORD,

than great treasure with trouble.

Better is a dinner of herbs, where love is,

than a fattened calf with hatred.

A wrathful man stirs up contention,

but one who is slow to anger appeases strife.

The way of the sluggard is like a thorn patch,

but the path of the upright is a highway.

A wise son makes a father glad,

but a foolish man despises his mother.

Folly is joy to one who is void of wisdom,

but a man of understanding keeps his way straight.

Where there is no counsel, plans fail;

but in a multitude of counselors they are established.

Joy comes to a man with the reply of his mouth.

How good is a word at the right time!

The path of life leads upward for the wise,

to keep him from going downward to Sheol.

the LORD will uproot the house of the proud,

but he will keep the widow's borders intact.

the LORD detests the thoughts of the wicked,

but the thoughts of the pure are pleasing.

He who is greedy for gain troubles his own house,

but he who hates bribes will live.

The heart of the righteous weighs answers,

but the mouth of the wicked gushes out evil.

THIRTY EIGHT

HAVE ENOUGH

"Better is little, with the fear of the LORD,
than great treasure with trouble." (PRO 15:16)

How much is really enough? What price are you paying for the extra you think you need? Is the ambition to be wealthier, fogging your focus on God? That is a key question. Please think about that for a moment. Don't dismiss it out of hand; it may apply to you.

Sometimes the price you pay is too much for the prize. What price are you paying? What price is your family paying? The price is often not the monetary amount but how much of your life you are willing to sacrifice in order to attain it.

Being grateful for what we already have can disempower the greed and consumerism that so easily ensnare us. Being content is a Godly attribute and reflects true priorities and a recognition that He has our best in mind.

> **QUICK PRAYER**: Thank You for what I already have, Lord. Amen.

the LORD is far from the wicked,

but he hears the prayer of the righteous.

The light of the eyes rejoices the heart.

Good news gives health to the bones.

The ear that listens to reproof lives,

and will be at home among the wise.

He who refuses correction despises his own soul,

but he who listens to reproof gets understanding.

The fear of the LORD teaches wisdom.

Before honor is humility.

THIRTY NINE
LISTEN

> *"Where there is no counsel, plans fail; but in a multitude of counselors they are established."* (PRO 15:22)

When we are in leadership, we often feel we need to be seen to have all the answers. Often we think we do have all the answers. The Scriptures are very clear that, despite our blind confidence, we don't. We need others' perspectives to get a holistic view. It is a call to humility that unlocks the collective wisdom in our organisations.

Often in our business as leaders we are removed from the reality of day-to-day contact with customers and suppliers. Those on the front line will often have massive insights into our problems and opportunities.

Even when identified, open dialogue and input are desirable for a clear view. Proverbs 19:20 emphasizes the point, saying, *"Listen to counsel and receive instruction, that you may be wise in your latter end"*.

QUICK PRAYER: Lord, help me to listen to those You have placed around me. Amen.

CHAPTER 16

The plans of the heart belong to man,
but the answer of the tongue is from the LORD.
All the ways of a man are clean in his own eyes;
but the LORD weighs the motives.

Commit your deeds to the LORD,
and your plans shall succeed.

the LORD has made everything for its own end—
yes, even the wicked for the day of evil.
Everyone who is proud in heart is an abomination to the LORD:
they shall certainly not be unpunished.
By mercy and truth iniquity is atoned for.
By the fear of the LORD men depart from evil.
When a man's ways please the LORD,
he makes even his enemies to be at peace with him.
Better is a little with righteousness,
than great revenues with injustice.

A man's heart plans his course,
but the LORD directs his steps.

Inspired judgments are on the lips of the king.
He shall not betray his mouth.
Honest balances and scales are the LORD's;
all the weights in the bag are his work.
It is an abomination for kings to do wrong,
for the throne is established by righteousness.
Righteous lips are the delight of kings.
They value one who speaks the truth.
The king's wrath is a messenger of death,
but a wise man will pacify it.

FORTY

ALIGNMENT

"Commit your deeds to The LORD, and
your plans shall succeed." (PRO 16:3)

If only my thoughts were aligned to God's will. Take a look at this Scripture. If we cast our works onto Him, commit and trust them to Him, He will make us think along the lines of His will. Why? So our plans will work and we will have success!

That is staggering in its significance. If we trust Him, He will turn our hearts to His will. We know that if we are in His will, He will guide us and lead us. How comforting it is to know that as we commit our works to Him, He will turn us to not only hear from Him, but our very thoughts will become His thoughts. Then we truly will have the mind of Christ.

How profound is this truth for leaders? We have the responsibility to lead others, how much more important for us to hear, commit and see our plans succeed.

> **QUICK PRAYER**: I commit my business to You. Please align my thoughts to Your will, that my plans may succeed. Amen.

In the light of the king's face is life.

His favor is like a cloud of the spring rain.

How much better it is to get wisdom than gold!

Yes, to get understanding is to be chosen rather than silver.

The highway of the upright is to depart from evil.

He who keeps his way preserves his soul.

Pride goes before destruction,

and a haughty spirit before a fall.

It is better to be of a lowly spirit with the poor,

than to divide the plunder with the proud.

He who heeds the Word finds prosperity.

Whoever trusts in the LORD is blessed.

The wise in heart shall be called prudent.

Pleasantness of the lips promotes instruction.

Understanding is a fountain of life to one who has it,

but the punishment of fools is their folly.

The heart of the wise instructs his mouth,

and adds learning to his lips.

Pleasant words are a honeycomb,

sweet to the soul, and health to the bones.

There is a way which seems right to a man,

but in the end it leads to death.

The appetite of the laboring man labors for him;

for his mouth urges him on.

A worthless man devises mischief.

His speech is like a scorching fire.

A perverse man stirs up strife.

A whisperer separates close friends.

FORTY ONE

CONTROL

"A man's heart plans his course, but The LORD directs his steps." (PRO 16:9)

If we have given our lives to God, He will guide our paths. What a reassurance that He is indeed in control. So should we stop planning? No, of course not. But in our planning, let's invite God to participate. He will anyway, so why not get an inside view? It can often be an easier journey.

Making room for God as leaders is not always easy. Sometimes we have to push into Him in order to hear and download His will. That sounds a little artificial but the Word exhorts us to search for wisdom as for hidden treasure, sometimes that just takes time and effort.

We will plan and push out in a direction, but it is God who will establish our steps, God who will watch over the direction, and ultimately He who will determine the way. I take a lot of comfort in that.

> **QUICK PRAYER**: Establish my steps according to Your Word, Lord. Amen.

A man of violence entices his neighbor,

and leads him in a way that is not good.

One who winks his eyes to plot perversities,

one who compresses his lips, is bent on evil.

Gray hair is a crown of glory.

It is attained by a life of righteousness.

One who is slow to anger is better than the mighty;

one who rules his spirit, than he who takes a city.

The lot is cast into the lap,

but its every decision is from the LORD.

FORTY TWO

CHANCE

"The lot is cast into the lap, but its every decision is from the LORD." (PRO 16:33)

When is chance just chance? Is fate really fate? Our self-centered nature demands a sense of self-reliance, where we can dictate our terms and influence and control our futures. The idea that there is a random universe that God asserts His influence over occasionally has an innate appeal.

When our companies or workplace seems to be being pushed around by circumstances we can trust and pray that God will make His influence known even when it looks purely like chance.

But the bad news, or should I say good news, is that God is in control—so much so that even when lots are cast, something we consider pure chance, He dictates the outcome. Just to emphasize the point, the Scripture tells us "its every decision" comes from Him. We might prefer an occasionally rather than an every, but get used to it—He is in control.

QUICK PRAYER: Thank You that what happens to me is not random but has purpose. Amen.

CHAPTER 17

B etter is a dry morsel with quietness,
than a house full of feasting with strife.

A servant who deals wisely will rule over a son who causes shame,

and shall have a part in the inheritance among the brothers.

The refining pot is for silver, and the furnace for gold,

but the LORD tests the hearts.

An evildoer heeds wicked lips.

A liar gives ear to a mischievous tongue.

Whoever mocks the poor reproaches his Maker.

He who is glad at calamity shall not be unpunished.

Children's children are the crown of old men;

the glory of children are their parents.

Arrogant speech isn't fitting for a fool,

much less do lying lips fit a prince.

A bribe is a precious stone in the eyes of him who gives it;

wherever he turns, he prospers.

He who covers an offense promotes love;

but he who repeats a matter separates best friends.

A rebuke enters deeper into one who has understanding

than a hundred lashes into a fool.

An evil man seeks only rebellion;

therefore a cruel messenger shall be sent against him.

Let a bear robbed of her cubs meet a man,

rather than a fool in his folly.

Whoever rewards evil for good,

evil shall not depart from his house.

The beginning of strife is like breaching a dam,

therefore stop contention before quarreling breaks out.

FORTY THREE

PRIORITIES

"Better is a dry morsel with quietness, than a house full of feasting with strife." (PRO 17:1)

What price do we put on success? What price will we pay for success? How do we measure it? Sometimes our worldly temporal view is clouded and shaped by the society we live in. Our worldview is influenced by the saturation of our cultural norms.

We live in a consumerist society, there is no escaping the western worldview that more is better; here is the shiny new thing you didn't know about yesterday, but now need today.

In this proverb it seemingly goes to extremes, at least from our Western perspective. Quietness is valued over plenty of food, as is peace, or more correctly 'lack of strife'.

It speaks to Godly priorities that don't match our worldly ones. When our priorities are wrong and we chase after more, it is our relationships, peace and tranquility that suffer. These are more highly prized by God than abundance, or even, dare I say, sufficiency.

> **QUICK PRAYER**: Thank you for your provision Lord, help me to keep my priorities in perspective. Amen.

He who justifies the wicked, and he who condemns the righteous,
both of them alike are an abomination to the LORD.
Why is there money in the hand of a fool to buy wisdom,
since he has no understanding?
A friend loves at all times;
and a brother is born for adversity.
A man void of understanding strikes hands,
and becomes collateral in the presence of his neighbor.
He who loves disobedience loves strife.
One who builds a high gate seeks destruction.
One who has a perverse heart doesn't find prosperity,
and one who has a deceitful tongue falls into trouble.
He who becomes the father of a fool grieves.
The father of a fool has no joy.
A cheerful heart makes good medicine,
but a crushed spirit dries up the bones.
A wicked man receives a bribe in secret,
to pervert the ways of justice.
Wisdom is before the face of one who has understanding,
but the eyes of a fool wander to the ends of the earth.
A foolish son brings grief to his father,
and bitterness to her who bore him.
Also to punish the righteous is not good,
nor to flog officials for their integrity.
He who spares his words has knowledge.
He who is even tempered is a man of understanding.
Even a fool, when he keeps silent, is counted wise.
When he shuts his lips, he is thought to be discerning.

FORTY FOUR

SCHMUCK

*"A man void of understanding strikes hands,
and becomes collateral in the presence of
his neighbor."* (PRO 17:18)

Someone, obviously of Jewish heritage, once said that a guarantor is just a "schmuck with a pen". Perhaps this is a somewhat unkind designation, yet quite possibly the sentiment of this Jewish gentleman agrees with the Word of God.

Don't put up security for a neighbor. If you have pledged for another, go now and unshackle yourself from potential disaster. Only you can meet the obligations you promise to another. You cannot guarantee the debts or behaviors of others.

In business we know that sometimes we have to provide collateral, but let us do so cognoscente of the view expressed above. Don't do it for others, don't do it at all if possible, or see it as a short term necessity, to be untangled from, at the earliest possible juncture.

God is quite clear, don't be a schmuck.

> **QUICK PRAYER**: Free me from pledges. Amen.

CHAPTER 18

An unfriendly man pursues selfishness,
and defies all sound judgment.
A fool has no delight in understanding,
but only in revealing his own opinion.
When wickedness comes, contempt also comes,
and with shame comes disgrace.
The words of a man's mouth are like deep waters.
The fountain of wisdom is like a flowing brook.
To be partial to the faces of the wicked is not good,
nor to deprive the innocent of justice.
A fool's lips come into strife,
and his mouth invites beatings.
A fool's mouth is his destruction,
and his lips are a snare to his soul.
The words of a gossip are like dainty morsels:
they go down into a person's innermost parts.
One who is slack in his work
is brother to him who is a master of destruction.
The name of the LORD is a strong tower:
the righteous run to him, and are safe.
The rich man's wealth is his strong city,
like an unscalable wall in his own imagination.
Before destruction the heart of man is proud,
but before honor is humility.
He who gives answer before he hears,
that is folly and shame to him.
A man's spirit will sustain him in sickness,
but a crushed spirit, who can bear?

FORTY FIVE

WORDS

> *"Death and life are in the power of the*
> *tongue; those who love it will eat its fruit."*
> (PRO 18:21)

You are what you say. God spoke the world into being, and we are created in His image. How many have been damaged by having negative words spoken over them by a parent, teacher, or minister?

Describing the tongue as having the power of life and death is about as strong a term as you could use. God is obviously placing a massive emphasis on the importance of what we say, so therefore, should we.

What do we say about our team, our company, our customers, our bosses, owners, suppliers or other stakeholders? Are we speaking life or death?

Watch what you say, be measured in your words, and encourage, build up, and edify those around you and yourself. You will inhabit the world created by your words.

QUICK PRAYER: Help me to be aware of my words and the power they hold. Amen.

The heart of the discerning gets knowledge.

The ear of the wise seeks knowledge.

A man's gift makes room for him,

and brings him before great men.

He who pleads his cause first seems right;

until another comes and questions him.

The lot settles disputes,

and keeps strong ones apart.

A brother offended is more difficult than a fortified city;

and disputes are like the bars of a castle.

A man's stomach is filled with the fruit of his mouth.

With the harvest of his lips he is satisfied.

Death and life are in the power of the tongue;

those who love it will eat its fruit.

Whoever finds a wife finds a good thing,

and obtains favor of the LORD.

The poor plead for mercy,

but the rich answer harshly.

A man of many companions may be ruined,

but there is a friend who sticks closer than a brother.

FORTY SIX

FRIENDS

"A man of many companions may be ruined, but there is a friend who sticks closer than a brother." (PRO 18:24)

Businesspeople tend to have a lot of acquaintances but not too many friends. Taking the time to build deeper friendships is a great investment. Character-full friends who will be with you regardless of circumstances have enormous value. Perhaps you too can be a friend like that and enrich someone else's life.

We are all busy, but when we take the time to invest in others, we find ourselves surrounded by friends. The ones who give and take, who love with reciprocity, who live transparently, and who will hold us in mutual accountability—those are our true friends.

Like all worthwhile things, true friendships develop over time, need care and consideration, and can endure the good times and the bad.

> **QUICK PRAYER**: Give me wisdom in my friendships please, Lord. Amen.

CHAPTER 19

Better is the poor who walks in his integrity
than he who is perverse in his lips and is a fool.

It isn't good to have zeal without knowledge;

nor being hasty with one's feet and missing the way.

The foolishness of man subverts his way;

his heart rages against the LORD.

Wealth adds many friends,

but the poor is separated from his friend.

A false witness shall not be unpunished.

He who pours out lies shall not go free.

Many will entreat the favor of a ruler,

and everyone is a friend to a man who gives gifts.

All the relatives of the poor shun him:

how much more do his friends avoid him!

He pursues them with pleas, but they are gone.

He who gets wisdom loves his own soul.

He who keeps understanding shall find good.

A false witness shall not be unpunished.

He who utters lies shall perish.

Delicate living is not appropriate for a fool,

much less for a servant to have rule over princes.

The discretion of a man makes him slow to anger.

It is his glory to overlook an offense.

The king's wrath is like the roaring of a lion,

but his favor is like dew on the grass.

A foolish son is the calamity of his father.

A wife's quarrels are a continual dripping.

FORTY SEVEN

HASTINESS

"It isn't good to have zeal without knowledge;
nor being hasty with one's feet and missing
the way." (PRO 19:2)

The business word is fast paced, changing rapidly, sometimes it is just a blur. As leaders we are called upon to make decisions quickly, remain flexible, innovative and spontaneous. But fast is not always best, and the first decision is not always the most prudent.

We can get caught up in the enthusiasm and fervor of a new initiative, change program or strategy. But if we have enthusiasm without a fair measure of facts, we could be hastening our demise. Equally, if we always make a quick judgment call or succumb to pressure for an answer, we may well be 'missing the way'.

Often others' deadlines are a measure of their lack of planning, rather than a need for immediacy. We can mistake speed for effectiveness, if we are not careful.

There is wisdom in taking time on important calls; that wisdom is often borne in collaboration with wise councilors. Sometimes more facts need to be brought to bear on the decision. What are the alternatives, have we looked at the risks? How can we make this decision an even better one?

There is a time for an instant response, but as this proverb reminds us, it is often wise to take time for some consideration.

QUICK PRAYER: Lord, help me to discern
between the urgent and the important. Amen.

House and riches are an inheritance from fathers,
but a prudent wife is from the LORD.
Slothfulness casts into a deep sleep.
The idle soul shall suffer hunger.
He who keeps the commandment keeps his soul,
but he who is contemptuous in his ways shall die.
He who has pity on the poor lends to the LORD;
he will reward him.
Discipline your son, for there is hope;
don't be a willing party to his death.
A hot-tempered man must pay the penalty,
for if you rescue him, you must do it again.
Listen to counsel and receive instruction,
that you may be wise in your latter end.
There are many plans in a man's heart,
but the LORD's counsel will prevail.
That which makes a man to be desired is his kindness.
A poor man is better than a liar.
The fear of the LORD leads to life, then contentment;
he rests and will not be touched by trouble.
The sluggard buries his hand in the dish;
he will not so much as bring it to his mouth again.
Flog a scoffer, and the simple will learn prudence;
rebuke one who has understanding, and he will gain knowledge.
He who robs his father and drives away his mother,
is a son who causes shame and brings reproach.
If you stop listening to instruction, my son,
you will stray from the words of knowledge.

FORTY EIGHT

DISCRETION

> *"The discretion of a man makes him slow to anger. It is his glory to overlook an offense."*
> (PRO 19:11)

Isn't it annoying when you ask someone to do something and they stuff it up? Maybe it's just me, but when someone is capable and they don't deliver, I can get a little short in my attitude. I am absolutely sure you don't react like this, but maybe you know someone who does?

Discretion is a wonderful attribute; one might even say Godly. To overlook an offence is to our glory. What a beautiful picture of grace and mercy. The Father overlooks all our sin because Jesus bore it when He died for us. How much more should we operate in grace and mercy to those around us. We know how much we need and rely on His mercy.

Let's endeavour to overlook offence and choose not to be offended. Let's operate in discretion and be slow to anger. I think people would like to work in a place like that. I think that people would like to work for a leader like that, I certainly would.

Jesus is, as always, our example; He shows us a way that is above our natural tendencies of judgment. He is transforming us into His image, so I am sure we will all have plenty of opportunity to exercise discretion.

QUICK PRAYER: I choose not to be offended because you are not offended by me. Amen.

A corrupt witness mocks justice,

and the mouth of the wicked gulps down iniquity.

Penalties are prepared for scoffers,

and beatings for the backs of fools.

FORTY NINE

HONESTY

> *"That which makes a man to be desired is his kindness. A poor man is better than a liar."*
> (PRO 19:22)

We all have an innate reaction that will cause us to protect ourselves when under threat. Our first response when we are accused is to deny. We learn to overcome this protective response though the conscious choice to operate in honesty and integrity.

At what point would we lie to save ourselves, or our finances? This is a tough question and one hopefully we won't need to know the answer to, but I would doubt many of us would refuse to say a little, tiny, insignificant white lie that wouldn't hurt a fly rather than lose all our finances, our house, car, job, and possessions.

The same is true in our leadership roles, what would it take for us to lie rather than take a financial penalty? Some say we all have a price, is that true?

God's view? It is better to be poor than a liar, and honesty is a mark of unfailing love.

QUICK PRAYER: Keep me honest above all things. Amen.

CHAPTER 20

Wine is a mocker, and beer is a brawler.
Whoever is led astray by them is not wise.
The terror of a king is like the roaring of a lion.
He who provokes him to anger forfeits his own life.
It is an honor for a man to keep aloof from strife;
but every fool will be quarreling.
The sluggard will not plow by reason of the winter;
therefore he shall beg in harvest, and have nothing.
Counsel in the heart of man is like deep water;
but a man of understanding will draw it out.
Many men claim to be men of unfailing love,
but who can find a faithful man?
A righteous man walks in integrity.
Blessed are his children after him.
A king who sits on the throne of judgment
scatters away all evil with his eyes.
Who can say, "I have made my heart pure.
I am clean and without sin?"
Differing weights and differing measures,
both of them alike are an abomination to the LORD.
Even a child makes himself known by his doings,
whether his work is pure, and whether it is right.
The hearing ear, and the seeing eye,
the LORD has made even both of them.
Don't love sleep, lest you come to poverty.
Open your eyes, and you shall be satisfied with bread.
"It's no good, it's no good," says the buyer;
but when he is gone his way, then he boasts.

FIFTY

BIG PRICE

"Fraudulent food is sweet to a man, but
afterwards his mouth is filled with gravel."
(PRO 20:17)

In leadership there is always a temptation to take the easy path. Often the easy answer has some inherent shortcuts or shortcomings. We can often justify this behavior by telling ourselves, "They will never know" or "It won't hurt anyone."

In the short term, it may even garner a good result. You may well get the quick win or the instant gratification. However, the Scripture here is very clear: in the longer term, there is always a price to pay for dishonesty or fraud.

Fraud doesn't have to be grand larceny; just some deception will be enough to meet the definition. A "mouth full of gravel" doesn't sound like an insignificant consequence ether. God's Word is to protect us, not to spoil the party.

> **QUICK PRAYER**: Keep me strictly honest in all my dealings. Amen.

There is gold and abundance of rubies;

but the lips of knowledge are a rare jewel.

Take the garment of one who puts up collateral for a stranger;

and hold him in pledge for a wayward woman.

Fraudulent food is sweet to a man,

but afterwards his mouth is filled with gravel.

Plans are established by advice;

by wise guidance you wage war!

He who goes about as a tale-bearer reveals secrets;

therefore don't keep company with him who opens wide his lips.

Whoever curses his father or his mother,

his lamp shall be put out in blackness of darkness.

An inheritance quickly gained at the beginning,

won't be blessed in the end.

Don't say, "I will pay back evil."

Wait for the LORD, and he will save you.

the LORD detests differing weights,

and dishonest scales are not pleasing.

A man's steps are from the LORD;

how then can man understand his way?

It is a snare to a man to make a rash dedication,

then later to consider his vows.

A wise king winnows out the wicked,

and drives the threshing wheel over them.

The spirit of man is the LORD's lamp,

searching all his innermost parts.

Love and faithfulness keep the king safe.

His throne is sustained by love.

FIFTY ONE

ADVISORS

> *"Plans are established by advice; by wise guidance you wage war!"* (PRO 20:18)

How often do you think you know best? Often we only think we are right because we haven't heard anything better. Perhaps there is a better way. Just because we lead doesn't mean we have all the answers and have to be infallible.

When we are embarking on a new venture, making a new plan, or moving in a new direction, there is wisdom in seeking the advice of others. It is pride or haste that stops us from seeking the wisdom of others. When we are reliant on ourselves, we are guaranteed to make the mistakes that others have already made.

There is often wisdom in the collective reasoning of a team of close advisers. Many brains are better than one. When we look at a problem or opportunity from a number of different perspectives, the conclusions we draw are more complete.

QUICK PRAYER: Keep me open to the guidance of others, Lord. Amen.

The glory of young men is their strength.
The splendor of old men is their gray hair.
Wounding blows cleanse away evil,
and beatings purge the innermost parts.

CHAPTER 21

**The king's heart is in the LORD's hand like the watercourses.
He turns it wherever he desires.**

Every way of a man is right in his own eyes,

but the LORD weighs the hearts.

To do righteousness and justice

is more acceptable to the LORD than sacrifice.

A high look, and a proud heart,

the lamp of the wicked, is sin.

The plans of the diligent surely lead to profit;

and everyone who is hasty surely rushes to poverty.

Getting treasures by a lying tongue

is a fleeting vapor for those who seek death.

The violence of the wicked will drive them away,

because they refuse to do what is right.

The way of the guilty is devious,

but the conduct of the innocent is upright.

It is better to dwell in the corner of the housetop,

than to share a house with a contentious woman.

The soul of the wicked desires evil;

his neighbor finds no mercy in his eyes.

When the mocker is punished, the simple gains wisdom.

When the wise is instructed, he receives knowledge.

The Righteous One considers the house of the wicked,

and brings the wicked to ruin.

Whoever stops his ears at the cry of the poor,

he will also cry out, but shall not be heard.

A gift in secret pacifies anger;

and a bribe in the cloak, strong wrath.

FIFTY TWO

KING'S HEART

> *"The king's heart is in The LORD's hand like the watercourses. He turns it wherever he desires."* (PRO 21:1)

God has the power to change a man's heart. He has the influence to give you favor amongst men and a willingness to open doors for His children. As His follower, you have a right to ask for His influence and favor. He may say no, or he may open a door that seems stuck fast.

Why not ask and see him empower you and your business as you seek to serve Him? The right favor and the right time can bring breakthrough change. Sometimes we look at an option and say, "That would never happen." But God is the God of the breakthrough, quite capable of moving a man's heart and giving you favor. Ask Him; you may be surprised at the outcome.

QUICK PRAYER: Lord, would you incline the heart of those in authority toward me, please?
Amen.

It is joy to the righteous to do justice;

but it is a destruction to the workers of iniquity.

The man who wanders out of the way of understanding

shall rest in the assembly of the dead.

He who loves pleasure shall be a poor man.

He who loves wine and oil shall not be rich.

The wicked is a ransom for the righteous;

the treacherous for the upright.

It is better to dwell in a desert land,

than with a contentious and fretful woman.

There is precious treasure and oil in the dwelling of the wise;

but a foolish man swallows it up.

He who follows after righteousness and kindness

finds life, righteousness, and honor.

A wise man scales the city of the mighty,

and brings down the strength of its confidence.

Whoever guards his mouth and his tongue

keeps his soul from troubles.

The proud and haughty man, "scoffer" is his name;

he works in the arrogance of pride.

The desire of the sluggard kills him,

for his hands refuse to labor.

There are those who covet greedily all day long;

but the righteous give and don't withhold.

The sacrifice of the wicked is an abomination:

how much more, when he brings it with a wicked mind!

A false witness will perish,

and a man who listens speaks to eternity.

FIFTY THREE

PLANS

> *"The plans of the diligent surely lead to profit; and everyone who is hasty surely rushes to poverty."* (PRO 21:5 NASB)

The old adage goes, "If you fail to plan, you plan to fail." Is it a cliché, yes, but it is nonetheless true, and the Scriptures agree. I have seen many business plans that have been so long and so complex that they are rendered useless. They go straight in someone's bottom drawer, only to see the light of day at the next 'strategic review.'

Planning in its purest sense is clearly identifying what you want to look like in the future. Take a view—say three years hence—and very clearly, and more importantly, demonstrably and empirically, write down in the simplest measurable terms what your business should look like. Then work out the simple steps to get there, and ensure your people are empowered to deliver their piece.

QUICK PRAYER: Lord, help me to plan, and as I commit these plans to You, bring them to pass according to Your Word. Thank You and amen.

A wicked man hardens his face;

but as for the upright, he establishes his ways.

There is no wisdom nor understanding

nor counsel against the LORD.

The horse is prepared for the day of battle;

but victory is with the LORD.

FIFTY FOUR

BIG PROBLEMS

> *"A wise man scales the city of the mighty, and*
> *brings down the strength of its confidence."*
> (PRO 21:22)

Every so often in business we face big problems. These are not the ordinary things of life but those massive, almost overwhelming problems that rarely impact us but that can be very intimidating. This is when we really need the wisdom of God. Let Him lay down the strategy, and in His strength you can overcome and pull down the mighty stronghold.

Take the time to wait on Him for an answer. Often a big problem causes an immediate response from us. We want to act because we feel doing nothing is ignoring the problem. Taking time to hear from God can result in a suitable response empowered by the God Who overcomes.

When the problem is big we have to rely on Him, knowing that only He can get us through. When it is overcome, God gets the glory and our faith grows knowing He has intervened on our behalf.

QUICK PRAYER: Give me the wisdom to overcome this big problem, Lord. Amen.

CHAPTER 22

A good name is more desirable than great riches,
and loving favor is better than silver and gold.
The rich and the poor have this in common:
the LORD is the maker of them all.
A prudent man sees danger, and hides himself;
but the simple pass on, and suffer for it.
The result of humility and the fear of the LORD
is wealth, honor, and life.
Thorns and snares are in the path of the wicked:
whoever guards his soul stays from them.
Train up a child in the way he should go,
and when he is old he will not depart from it.
The rich rule over the poor.
The borrower is servant to the lender.
He who sows wickedness reaps trouble,
and the rod of his fury will be destroyed.
He who has a generous eye will be blessed;
for he shares his food with the poor.
Drive out the mocker, and strife will go out;
yes, quarrels and insults will stop.
He who loves purity of heart and speaks gracefully
is the king's friend.
The eyes of the LORD watch over knowledge;
but he frustrates the words of the unfaithful.
The sluggard says, "There is a lion outside!
I will be killed in the streets!"
The mouth of an adulteress is a deep pit:
he who is under the LORD's wrath will fall into it.

FIFTY FIVE

GOOD NAME

> *"A good name is more desirable than great riches, and loving favor is better than silver and gold."* (PRO 22:1)

Avoiding shortcuts and not burning bridges are two ways of protecting your reputation. Being pleasant to deal with, regardless of how difficult a situation or how bad a deal goes, will ensure your reputation stays in place.

Being a leader we will rise or fall on our reputations. Leadership is not an excuse to lord it over others, it is a position from which to serve both individuals and organizations. How we do so will determine our reputation.

The Bible places such things above material gain and above precious jewels. We too should have the same perspective. We are the physical manifestation of God's love to the world, after all. Often people will judge God by how they see us.

Protecting our reputation protects God's reputation; we are, after all, His representatives.

QUICK PRAYER: Please protect my reputation.
Amen.

Folly is bound up in the heart of a child:

the rod of discipline drives it far from him.

Whoever oppresses the poor for his own increase and whoever

gives to the rich,

both come to poverty.

Turn your ear, and listen to the words of the wise.

Apply your heart to my teaching.

For it is a pleasant thing if you keep them within you,

if all of them are ready on your lips.

That your trust may be in the LORD,

I teach you today, even you.

Haven't I written to you thirty excellent things

of counsel and knowledge,

To teach you truth, reliable words,

to give sound answers to the ones who sent you?

Don't exploit the poor, because he is poor;

and don't crush the needy in court;

for the LORD will plead their case,

and plunder the life of those who plunder them.

Don't befriend a hot-tempered man,

and don't associate with one who harbors anger:

lest you learn his ways,

and ensnare your soul.

FIFTY SIX

SLAVERY

> *"The rich rule over the poor. The borrower is
> servant to the lender."* (PRO 22:7)

I don't think I would like to be a slave. Despite us thinking that it is an ancient trade, there are more slaves on the planet today than there have ever been. It is a tragic industry trading in human misery.

Yet here in Proverbs, a borrower is described as a slave to the lender. The power a master has over a slave has no end. It is a good reminder about God's attitude toward debt. When we are in debt, we are literally owned by the person we are in debt to. Think twice and think again before entering into debt.

What is true for the individual is true for our organizations. Debt comes with a price that is higher than the sticker; it moves us into a beholden situation and we would do well to be mindful of the consequences.

Give due heed to this Scripture when you look to enter into any debt contract. When we are in debt, we lose a piece of our freedom.

QUICK PRAYER: Teach me how to live with minimal debt. Amen.

Don't you be one of those who strike hands,
of those who are collateral for debts.
If you don't have means to pay,
why should he take away your bed from under you?

Don't move the ancient boundary stone,
which your fathers have set up.

Do you see a man skilled in his work?
He will serve kings.
He won't serve obscure men.

FIFTY SEVEN

OBSCURITY

"Do you see a man skilled in his work? He
will serve kings. He won't serve obscure men."
(PRO 22:29)

We are all given a fixed amount of gifts and talents. They are allocated for a purpose, in that we all have a role to play and a part to fulfill. They do come, however, with some responsibility.

Raw talent can only get us so far as leaders. The one with some talent will go way past the one with much unless the one with more learns diligence and applies him or herself. We are called to take what God has given us and to hone and develop it with the gifts He has bestowed on us.

Training and learning are not self-interest pastimes; they are the building blocks of servanthood. If we are well equipped and prepared, we can serve effectively and be productive. Then we will be taken to new heights and given even greater opportunity to serve.

> **QUICK PRAYER**: I commit to developing the skills
> You have given me so I may serve You well.
> Amen.

CHAPTER 23

When you sit to eat with a ruler,
consider diligently what is before you;
put a knife to your throat,
if you are a man given to appetite.
Don't be desirous of his dainties,
since they are deceitful food.
Don't weary yourself to be rich.
In your wisdom, show restraint.
Why do you set your eyes on that which is not?
For it certainly sprouts wings like an eagle and flies in the sky.
Don't eat the food of him who has a stingy eye,
and don't crave his delicacies:
for as he thinks about the cost, so he is.
"Eat and drink!" he says to you,
but his heart is not with you.
The morsel which you have eaten you shall vomit up,
and lose your good words.

Don't speak in the ears of a fool,
for he will despise the wisdom of your words.

Don't move the ancient boundary stone.
Don't encroach on the fields of the fatherless:
for their Defender is strong.
He will plead their case against you.

Apply your heart to instruction,
and your ears to the words of knowledge.

FIFTY EIGHT

BREAKTHROUGH

"Indeed surely there is a future hope, and your hope will not be cut off." (PRO 23:18)

Sometimes life is tough—often very tough. Leadership can bring extra pressures of responsibility for others and the organisation or team. But we serve a God who is a Redeemer.

Regardless of what you face today, there is hope in God; Even self-inflicted trouble can be redeemed by Him. It seems to be the most common kind of trouble.

King David, the adulterer and murderer who took another man's wife and had her husband killed, was forgiven and his situation redeemed. The fruit of this relationship was Solomon, the greatest and wisest of all men. God created a future and hope and was David's salvation.

There is a future, and God loves you, cares about you, and died for you. He still has a plan and purpose for your life, regardless of your circumstances.

> **QUICK PRAYER**: Thank You for hope. You are my salvation. Amen.

Don't withhold correction from a child.

If you punish him with the rod, he will not die.

Punish him with the rod,

and save his soul from Sheol.

My son, if your heart is wise,

then my heart will be glad, even mine:

yes, my heart will rejoice,

when your lips speak what is right.

Don't let your heart envy sinners;

but rather fear the LORD all the day long.

Indeed surely there is a future hope,

and your hope will not be cut off.

Listen, my son, and be wise,

and keep your heart on the right path!

Don't be among ones drinking too much wine,

or those who gorge themselves on meat:

for the drunkard and the glutton shall become poor;

and drowsiness clothes them in rags.

Listen to your father who gave you life,

and don't despise your mother when she is old.

Buy the truth, and don't sell it.

Get wisdom, discipline, and understanding.

The father of the righteous has great joy.

Whoever fathers a wise child delights in him.

Let your father and your mother be glad!

Let her who bore you rejoice!

FIFTY NINE

PARENTS

> *"Listen to your father who gave you life, and*
> *don't despise your mother when she is old."*
> (PRO 23:22)

Sometimes we assume that the parents' role is over when the child leaves home. Perhaps we would do well to heed the advice of the Bible that seems to honor a parent's advice for a lot longer time.

Just because you are now in a position of honour as a leader doesn't mean that we are freed from this obligation. It is just as applicable now as it was when we started out.

While we may not understand this principle, depending on our skill base and the relationship we have with our parents, it is nonetheless a God-ordained decree. They have a lot more life under their belts than we do, and while we may or may not respect their opinions, we would do well to open our ears to their advice based on this principle in God's Word.

> **QUICK PRAYER**: Keep me open to my parents' advice. Amen.

My son, give me your heart;

and let your eyes keep in my ways.

For a prostitute is a deep pit;

and a wayward wife is a narrow well.

Yes, she lies in wait like a robber,

and increases the unfaithful among men.

Who has woe?

Who has sorrow?

Who has strife?

Who has complaints?

Who has needless bruises?

Who has bloodshot eyes?

Those who stay long at the wine;

those who go to seek out mixed wine.

Don't look at the wine when it is red,

when it sparkles in the cup,

when it goes down smoothly.

In the end, it bites like a snake,

and poisons like a viper.

Your eyes will see strange things,

and your mind will imagine confusing things.

Yes, you will be as he who lies down in the midst of the sea,

or as he who lies on top of the rigging:

"They hit me, and I was not hurt!

They beat me, and I don't feel it!

When will I wake up? I can do it again.

I can find another."

CHAPTER 24

Don't be envious of evil men;
neither desire to be with them:
for their hearts plot violence,
and their lips talk about mischief.
Through wisdom a house is built;
by understanding it is established;
by knowledge the rooms are filled
with all rare and beautiful treasure.
A wise man has great power;
and a knowledgeable man increases strength;
for by wise guidance you wage your war;
and victory is in many advisors.
Wisdom is too high for a fool:
he doesn't open his mouth in the gate.
One who plots to do evil
will be called a schemer.
The schemes of folly are sin.
The mocker is detested by men.
If you falter in the time of trouble,
your strength is small.
Rescue those who are being led away to death!
Indeed, hold back those who are staggering to the slaughter!
If you say, "Behold, we didn't know this";
doesn't he who weighs the hearts consider it?
He who keeps your soul, doesn't he know it?
Shall he not render to every man according to his work?
My son, eat honey, for it is good;
the droppings of the honeycomb, which are sweet to your taste:

SIXTY

RESCUE

"Rescue those who are being led away to death! Indeed, hold back those who are staggering to the slaughter!" (PRO 24:11)

If we look forward and imagine ourselves in 100 years, make that 1000 years, what will have been important here on Earth? In our brief time here, insignificant in the light of an eternal perspective, what really matters?

Only those things we do that have eternal significance will impact for eternity. That sounds like a circular argument but it is nonetheless true. When we are on our deathbeds we will not be wishing we had spent more time at work; rather we will be looking to see if we have loved and lived; relationships will be paramount.

When we are in heaven, as all who trust Jesus will be, then we will wish we had done more to reach those around us. Suddenly all will become clear; it was not about what others thought about us, our careers, cars, houses, holidays or whatever. It was all about those things we did for the glory of God; those decisions we made in line with His will, which impacted others for Him.

The only thing we can take into Heaven is the souls of those who have seen our walk, heard our message and accepted our Saviour. You maybe their only hope and the consequences are literally horrific.

> **QUICK PRAYER:** Help me to reach someone today with you message Lord. Amen.

so you shall know wisdom to be to your soul;

if you have found it, then there will be a reward,

your hope will not be cut off.

Don't lay in wait, wicked man, against the habitation of the

righteous.

Don't destroy his resting place:

for a righteous man falls seven times, and rises up again;

but the wicked are overthrown by calamity.

Don't rejoice when your enemy falls.

Don't let your heart be glad when he is overthrown;

lest the LORD see it, and it displease him,

and he turn away his wrath from him.

Don't fret yourself because of evildoers;

neither be envious of the wicked:

for there will be no reward to the evil man;

and the lamp of the wicked shall be snuffed out.

My son, fear the LORD and the king.

Don't join those who are rebellious:

for their calamity will rise suddenly;

the destruction from them both—who knows?

These also are sayings of the wise.

To show partiality in judgment is not good.

He who says to the wicked, "You are righteous";

peoples shall curse him, and nations shall abhor him—

but it will go well with those who convict the guilty,

and a rich blessing will come on them.

SIXTY ONE

GET OUTSIDE

"Prepare your work outside, and get your fields ready. Afterwards, build your house."
(PRO 24:27)

There is a lot of wisdom in this one very short verse. When we approach a new problem or situation at work , we have to ascertain the priorities. In this case, part of the required solution is productive and will ensure the secondary outcome.

If the fields are planted and the income is assured, then time and resources can be allocated to building the house. If the approach is the opposite, the house may well be built but with no food and resources, and disaster would ensue. The outcome could well be the loss of the house.

These two outcomes—failure and success—came from the same set of resources in the same situation with the same people; the only differentiator was the priorities set.

A key leadership responsibility is to set priorities to ensure the sustainability of the entirety, not just a single project. We are the keepers of the vision and have the big picture. Knowing the priorities is at the core of good leadership.

QUICK PRAYER: I see Your priorities, Lord. Help me to align my life to them. Amen.

An honest answer
is like a kiss on the lips.
Prepare your work outside,
and get your fields ready.
Afterwards, build your house.
Don't be a witness against your neighbor without cause.
Don't deceive with your lips.
Don't say, "I will do to him as he has done to me;
I will render to the man according to his work."
I went by the field of the sluggard,
by the vineyard of the man void of understanding;
Behold, it was all grown over with thorns.
Its surface was covered with nettles,
and its stone wall was broken down.
Then I saw, and considered well.
I saw, and received instruction:
a little sleep, a little slumber,
a little folding of the hands to sleep;
so your poverty will come as a robber,
and your want as an armed man.

SIXTY TWO

SLEEP DEPRIVATION

"Then I saw, and considered well. I saw, and
received instruction: a little sleep, a little slumber,
a little folding of the hands to sleep; so your
poverty will come as a robber, and your want as
an armed man. (PRO 24:32-34)

I'm not a big fan of poverty. I certainly don't see it as some kind of sanctified state. We endeavour to address it in other lands and where it exists in our own countries. But sometimes lack hits a lot closer to home.

Riches, wealth or even just sustainable provision can be an illusion of certainty. I have seen it often in business, where good companies failed to address issues based on a false illusion of their own right to exist. They became lazy.

Poverty and want here in this proverb come as a robber or an armed man. Intruders and vagabonds operate suddenly. We don't see an armed man crawling slowly toward us over a week or two. Robbery is a sudden event.

So what can cause this 'sudden downfall' in our lives, our teams and our organisations? A little sleep, a little slumber, maybe a little rest. We can easily be lulled into a false sense of security and then suddenly.......

We need to be mindful that we have an enemy and that he too has a plan. To overcome this strategy we need to do the opposite. Stay alert, don't become complacent, remain diligent and apply ourselves in excellence at work, for the glory of God.

> **QUICK PRAYER**: Keep me diligent, awake and
> aware of the plans of the enemy. Amen.

CHAPTER 25

These also are proverbs of Solomon, which the men of Hezekiah
king of Judah copied out.

It is the glory of God to conceal a thing,
but the glory of kings is to search out a matter.
As the heavens for height, and the earth for depth,
so the hearts of kings are unsearchable.
Take away the dross from the silver,
and material comes out for the refiner;
Take away the wicked from the king's presence,
and his throne will be established in righteousness.
Don't exalt yourself in the presence of the king,
or claim a place among great men;
for it is better that it be said to you, "Come up here,"
than that you should be put lower in the presence of the prince,
whom your eyes have seen.
Don't be hasty in bringing charges to court.
What will you do in the end when your neighbor shames you?
Debate your case with your neighbor,
and don't betray the confidence of another;
lest one who hears it put you to shame,
and your bad reputation never depart.

A word fitly spoken
is like apples of gold in settings of silver.
As an earring of gold, and an ornament of fine gold,
so is a wise reprover to an obedient ear.

SIXTY THREE

EXALTATION

> *"Don't exalt yourself in the presence of the king,*
> *or claim a place among great men; for it is better*
> *that it be said to you, "Come up here," than that*
> *you should be put lower in the presence of the*
> *prince, whom your eyes have seen.* (PRO 25:6-7)

We all know them don't we? The puffed up, the proud the arrogant and the 'look at me'. Actually there is probably just enough of that in all of us to take a look at the advice in this proverb.

Let others exalt you rather than yourself. If you take the opportunity to show off and pull rank, you might just be put down by a bigger fish. There is always a bigger better fish in town.

Media tycoon Kerry Packer is famously quoted for an exchange in a poker tournament at the Stratosphere Casino, where a Texan oil investor was playing a game of poker. Upon the Texan saying "I'm worth $60 Million Packer apparently pulled out a coin and nonchalantly said "I'll toss you for it".

If we hold our lives, and what we have, with a little humility, it will serve us well. We know that we are nothing without Jesus. If we take the humble option, often we get exulted. God's Kingdom is like that.

QUICK PRAYER: Help me not to be too proud of my humility. Amen.

As the cold of snow in the time of harvest,
so is a faithful messenger to those who send him;
for he refreshes the soul of his masters.
As clouds and wind without rain,
so is he who boasts of gifts deceptively.
By patience a ruler is persuaded.
A soft tongue breaks the bone.
Have you found honey?
Eat as much as is sufficient for you,
lest you eat too much, and vomit it.
Let your foot be seldom in your neighbor's house,
lest he be weary of you, and hate you.
A man who gives false testimony against his neighbor
is like a club, a sword, or a sharp arrow.
Confidence in someone unfaithful in time of trouble
is like a bad tooth, or a lame foot.
As one who takes away a garment in cold weather,
or vinegar on soda,
so is one who sings songs to a heavy heart.
If your enemy is hungry, give him food to eat.
If he is thirsty, give him water to drink:
for you will heap coals of fire on his head,
and the LORD will reward you.
The north wind brings forth rain:
so a backbiting tongue brings an angry face.
It is better to dwell in the corner of the housetop,
than to share a house with a contentious woman.
Like cold water to a thirsty soul,
so is good news from a far country.

SIXTY FOUR

REFRESHING

"As the cold of snow in the time of harvest,
so is a faithful messenger to those who send
him; for he refreshes the soul of his masters."
(PRO 25:13)

A cold, crisp, refreshing drink after a hard day's labor is one of life's simple and rewarding pleasures. In this Scripture, that feeling of being refreshed and satisfied is compared to a faithful person who serves us at work.

We all know how great it is to find someone who is motivated and capable who can get on with a job and do excellent work. It is refreshing to see and experience excellence in a task assigned to someone.

Likewise, we should refresh those who have entrusted a task to us. If we operate with excellence and integrity, we will be a blessing to those in authority over us. We are also more likely to be blessed if we are a refreshing blessing.

QUICK PRAYER: Let me refresh those around me. Amen.

Like a muddied spring, and a polluted well,
so is a righteous man who gives way before the wicked.
It is not good to eat much honey;
nor is it honorable to seek one's own honor.
Like a city that is broken down and without walls
is a man whose spirit is without restraint.

SIXTY FIVE

COMPROMISE

> *"Like a muddied spring, and a polluted well,*
> *so is a righteous man who gives way before*
> *the wicked."* (PRO 25:26)

Pressure pressure pressure. Leaders are 'under the pump' all the time. There is an enormous amount of pressure for leaders in today's commercial environment. We are pushed and pulled by many stakeholders with a multitude of agendas.

If we have a foundation in Christ we have a resource we can call on. We will know what is right and what is wrong, and have the strength to make the right and occasionally unpopular decision.

People are watching and so is our God. Will we do the right thing, or will we cave to pressure, convenience or temptation? We all sometimes get it wrong and no man is without sin, but we should strive to endure under pressure, and make the righteous choice.

Don't give way before the wicked. Not only must you maintain a right course, it is a testimony before the angels, as you choose to do what is right even at personal cost. If you give way, the pure water of your testimony and life is muddied and sullied like a polluted well. Strong words; stay strong.

QUICK PRAYER: Keep me strong Lord. Amen

CHAPTER 26

Like snow in summer, and as rain in harvest,
so honor is not fitting for a fool.
Like a fluttering sparrow,
like a darting swallow,
so the undeserved curse doesn't come to rest.
A whip is for the horse,
a bridle for the donkey,
and a rod for the back of fools!
Don't answer a fool according to his folly,
lest you also be like him.
Answer a fool according to his folly,
lest he be wise in his own eyes.
One who sends a message by the hand of a fool
is cutting off feet and drinking violence.
Like the legs of the lame that hang loose:
so is a parable in the mouth of fools.
As one who binds a stone in a sling,
so is he who gives honor to a fool.
Like a thornbush that goes into the hand of a drunkard,
so is a parable in the mouth of fools.
As an archer who wounds all,
so is he who hires a fool
or he who hires those who pass by.
As a dog that returns to his vomit,
so is a fool who repeats his folly.
Do you see a man wise in his own eyes?
There is more hope for a fool than for him.
The sluggard says, "There is a lion in the road!
A fierce lion roams the streets!"

SIXTY SIX

HIRE SLOW

"As an archer who wounds all, so is he who hires a fool or he who hires those who pass by." (PRO 26:10)

There is a saying in business that we should hire slow and fire fast. There is actually a lot of truth in what seems like a flippant and perhaps ruthless saying. Like a lot of clichés, they exist because they are true.

Taking the time to ensure that the people we hire are suitable goes way beyond their resume. Yes, we need to hire someone who is able to technically fulfill the positions requirements, but if we value culture, we will go way beyond that.

Great companies are built on certain values and operate in a particular way. If we do not take these soft attributes into account, we will find that the good technical fit may actually be divisive and counterproductive to the whole.

If we hire on attitude and cultural fit, aptitude becomes a less important ingredient of success. Choose wisely if you want to be successful. We as leaders are only as good as those around us.

QUICK PRAYER: Remind me to hire slow. Amen.

As the door turns on its hinges,

so does the sluggard on his bed.

The sluggard buries his hand in the dish.

He is too lazy to bring it back to his mouth.

The sluggard is wiser in his own eyes

than seven men who answer with discretion.

Like one who grabs a dog's ears

is one who passes by and meddles in a quarrel not his own.

Like a madman who shoots torches, arrows, and death,

is the man who deceives his neighbor and says, "Am I not joking?"

For lack of wood a fire goes out.

Without gossip, a quarrel dies down.

As coals are to hot embers,

and wood to fire,

so is a contentious man to kindling strife.

The words of a whisperer are as dainty morsels,

they go down into the innermost parts.

Like silver dross on an earthen vessel

are the lips of a fervent one with an evil heart.

A malicious man disguises himself with his lips,

but he harbors evil in his heart.

When his speech is charming, don't believe him;

for there are seven abominations in his heart.

His malice may be concealed by deception,

but his wickedness will be exposed in the assembly.

Whoever digs a pit shall fall into it.

Whoever rolls a stone, it will come back on him.

A lying tongue hates those it hurts;

and a flattering mouth works ruin.

SIXTY SEVEN

DOG BITE

> *"Like one who grabs a dog's ears is one who
> passes by and meddles in a quarrel not his
> own."* (PRO 26:17)

I have a dog, a Staffordshire bull terrier. It looks mean enough to cause people to 'cross by on the other side'. We know it is really a pacifist and would rather run than fight, and is a bit of a softie. But don't grab it by the ears, she gets quite irate.

Why would you do that, grab a dog by the ears? It serves no purpose other than to make the recipient angry. A less tolerate dog than ours would get very aggressive and could do you some damage.

This proverb equated this behaviour with meddling in a quarrel not your own. That sounds quite extreme, but we are to listen to God's wisdom. It is written for a reason, to guide us and lead us.

Next time you are tempted to get nosy and interfere in someone else's quarrel, remember this piece of advice: don't. It will serve you well and could save you a lot of strife.

> **QUICK PRAYER:** Keep me from meddling Lord.
> Amen.

CHAPTER 27

Don't boast about tomorrow;

for you don't know what a day may bring forth.

Let another man praise you,

and not your own mouth;

a stranger, and not your own lips.

A stone is heavy,

and sand is a burden;

but a fool's provocation is heavier than both.

Wrath is cruel,

and anger is overwhelming;

but who is able to stand before jealousy?

Better is open rebuke

than hidden love.

Faithful are the wounds of a friend;

although the kisses of an enemy are profuse.

A full soul loathes a honeycomb;

but to a hungry soul, every bitter thing is sweet.

As a bird that wanders from her nest,

so is a man who wanders from his home.

Perfume and incense bring joy to the heart;

so does earnest counsel from a man's friend.

Don't forsake your friend and your father's friend.

Don't go to your brother's house in the day of your disaster:

better is a neighbor who is near than a distant brother.

Be wise, my son,

and bring joy to my heart,

then I can answer my tormentor.

A prudent man sees danger and takes refuge;

SIXTY EIGHT

SHARP

"Iron sharpens iron; so a man sharpens his friend's countenance." (PRO 27:17)

Who keeps you sharp? Who do you have in your life that you trust—whom you can "do life with"? We all need people who love God who can keep us sharp.

Leaders in particular can become very isolated and insular. We have to ensure we are actively looking at ways to address this deficit, in order to be at our best.

Often in our busy lives those relationships have drifted away or may not even exist. Ask God today to bring someone into your life or reacquaint yourself with a true friend. Why not schedule in some time to stay sharp with good company?

Be careful of a life with many acquaintances and no true friends. We all need some accountability. In order to gain true friendship, we need to be a true friend. As in any relationship, we will only get out what we put in. Investing in friendship is a sure way to surround yourself with great friends.

> **QUICK PRAYER**: Lead me to people who I can trust, Lord. Amen.

but the simple pass on, and suffer for it.

Take his garment when he puts up collateral for a stranger.

Hold it for a wayward woman!

He who blesses his neighbor with a loud voice early in the morning,

it will be taken as a curse by him.

A continual dropping on a rainy day

and a contentious wife are alike:

restraining her is like restraining the wind,

or like grasping oil in his right hand.

Iron sharpens iron;

so a man sharpens his friend's countenance.

Whoever tends the fig tree shall eat its fruit.

He who looks after his master shall be honored.

As water reflects a face,

so a man's heart reflects the man.

Sheol and Abaddon are never satisfied;

and a man's eyes are never satisfied.

The crucible is for silver,

and the furnace for gold;

but man is refined by his praise.

Though you grind a fool in a mortar with a pestle along with grain,

yet his foolishness will not be removed from him.

Know well the state of your flocks,

and pay attention to your herds:

for riches are not forever,

SIXTY NINE

PROTECT IT

> *"Whoever tends the fig tree shall eat its fruit. He who looks after his master shall be honored."* (PRO 27:18)

When we are given responsibility at work we need to receive it with a sense of responsibility. If we treat it well, as if it were our own, it will bear fruit.

When we protect the areas we are given with integrity and excellence, they will prosper. The byproduct of this is that we will actually be blessed by what we protect. He who guards the tree will eat of its fruit. Not only will that north and grow us it is accompanied with honour, this builds our reputation which in turn grows our capacity and opportunity.

We are called to be responsible regardless of the size of the task we are given. As we are faithful with the little we are given more; it is a spiritual law with natural consequences.

Plus, as we operate in a spirit of protection we will be given more responsibility because we will be deemed trustworthy by God and man.

QUICK PRAYER: Give me a spirit of preservation and protection. Amen.

nor does even the crown endure to all generations.
The hay is removed, and the new growth appears,
the grasses of the hills are gathered in.
The lambs are for your clothing,
and the goats are the price of a field.
There will be plenty of goats' milk for your food,
for your family's food,
and for the nourishment of your servant girls.

CHAPTER 28

The wicked flee when no one pursues;
but the righteous are as bold as a lion.
In rebellion, a land has many rulers,
but order is maintained by a man of understanding and knowledge.
A needy man who oppresses the poor
is like a driving rain which leaves no crops.
Those who forsake the law praise the wicked;
but those who keep the law contend with them.
Evil men don't understand justice;
but those who seek the LORD understand it fully.
Better is the poor who walks in his integrity,
than he who is perverse in his ways, and he is rich.
Whoever keeps the law is a wise son;
but he who is a companion of gluttons shames his father.
He who increases his wealth by excessive interest
gathers it for one who has pity on the poor.
He who turns away his ear from hearing the law,
even his prayer is an abomination.
Whoever causes the upright to go astray in an evil way,
he will fall into his own trap;
but the blameless will inherit good.
The rich man is wise in his own eyes;
but the poor who has understanding sees through him.
When the righteous triumph, there is great glory;
but when the wicked rise, men hide themselves.
He who conceals his sins doesn't prosper,
but whoever confesses and renounces them finds mercy.
Blessed is the man who always fears;
but one who hardens his heart falls into trouble.

SEVENTY

MERCY

"He who conceals his sins doesn't prosper, but whoever confesses and renounces them finds mercy." (PRO 28:13)

One of the down sides of an omnipotent God is that He sees everything. We have nowhere to hide. In fact, He knows what we are going to do even before we do it. Every dumb, crazy thing we will choose to do between now and when we die He is already fully aware of. We cannot surprise Him in any way.

So if we fall, let's not find a dark corner and have a pity party; let's not get into condemnation, saying, "God can never use me." Let's not stop meeting with Him as we wallow in our own disappointment and pride.

God has already forgiven you. He provided full pardon at the cross for all the sins of all men for all time. It is finished. Confess your sin, receive God's mercy, and move on.

QUICK PRAYER: Thank You for Your mercy, Jesus. Amen.

As a roaring lion or a charging bear,

so is a wicked ruler over helpless people.

A tyrannical ruler lacks judgment.

One who hates ill-gotten gain will have long days.

A man who is tormented by life blood will be a fugitive until death;

no one will support him.

Whoever walks blamelessly is kept safe;

but one with perverse ways will fall suddenly.

One who works his land will have an abundance of food;

but one who chases fantasies will have his fill of poverty.

A faithful man is rich with blessings;

but one who is eager to be rich will not go unpunished.

To show partiality is not good;

yet a man will do wrong for a piece of bread.

A stingy man hurries after riches,

and doesn't know that poverty waits for him.

One who rebukes a man will afterward find more favor

than one who flatters with the tongue.

Whoever robs his father or his mother, and says, "It's not wrong."

He is a partner with a destroyer.

One who is greedy stirs up strife;

but one who trusts in the LORD will prosper.

One who trusts in himself is a fool;

but one who walks in wisdom is kept safe.

One who gives to the poor has no lack;

but one who closes his eyes will have many curses.

When the wicked rise, men hide themselves;

but when they perish, the righteous thrive.

SEVENTY ONE

REBUKE

> *"One who rebukes a man will afterward find more favor than one who flatters with the tongue."* (PRO 28:23)

I am not sure why, or when it started, but we have a false view of what it is to be 'Christian'. We have equated it with being 'nice'. It is such an awfully insipid weak word. But it is true; we have taken the rugged Carpenter and turned Him into an effeminate pale apparition. We have taken on a distorted shadow.

Sometimes we are called on to be tough, and to call it as we see it. Sometimes we are required to bring light to darkness, and salt can be an astringent and a disinfectant. Can we rebuke? Yes, in love, with wisdom, and a heart to reconcile and bring good fruit.

The easy option is to flatter the ears of men rather than follow the call of God and intervene for good. Take the narrow road and you may win a friend for life, redeem a lost soul, or uncover the potential resident in a team member.

Encourage and complement, don't flatter, Rebuke in love and wisdom, don't crush and cut with your tongue. If you learn the difference you will be wise and effective.

QUICK PRAYER: Give me the wisdom, heart and strength to confront and rebuke when necessary Lord. Amen.

CHAPTER 29

He who is often rebuked and stiffens his neck
will be destroyed suddenly, with no remedy.
When the righteous thrive, the people rejoice;
but when the wicked rule, the people groan.
Whoever loves wisdom brings joy to his father;
but a companion of prostitutes squanders his wealth.
The king by justice makes the land stable,
but he who takes bribes tears it down.
A man who flatters his neighbor
spreads a net for his feet.
An evil man is snared by his sin,
but the righteous can sing and be glad.
The righteous care about justice for the poor.
The wicked aren't concerned about knowledge.
Mockers stir up a city,
but wise men turn away anger.
If a wise man goes to court with a foolish man,
the fool rages or scoffs, and there is no peace.
The bloodthirsty hate a man of integrity;
and they seek the life of the upright.
A fool vents all of his anger,
but a wise man brings himself under control.
If a ruler listens to lies,
all of his officials are wicked.
The poor man and the oppressor have this in common:
the LORD gives sight to the eyes of both.
The king who fairly judges the poor,
his throne shall be established forever.

SEVENTY TWO

COURT JESTER

> *"If a wise man goes to court with a foolish man, the fool rages or scoffs, and there is no peace.* (PRO 29:9)

Here is a very tough one for you to consider. There is definitely a time to seek legal recourse when it is necessary to do so. Certainly though, it is a means of last resort. This is particularly true when the offending party may be a believer.

We are exhorted to find all means to settle a matter before it goes to court, even finding counsel and hopefully reconciliation in the church, before making it a public and legal matter.

Occasionally we are up against a fool, one who will rage and scoff and cause undue trouble. Even when we are in the right and have a case, we still need to go to God and seek His wisdom. Do I exercise my rights and seek what is due to me, or do I walk away?

I've been here, and it is a very difficult decision. If I don't pursue then what will they learn, they've got away with it again! ? Someone needs to each them a lesson. It can easily become an exercise in judgment rather than seeking a fair outcome. This proverb wisely says there is a time to walk away from a foolish man, and let God balance the scales as He sees fit. Choosing peace over a raging and scoffing fool is not weakness; it's wisdom.

QUICK PRAYER: I forgive those who have wronged me, and leave them in your hands Lord. Amen.

The rod of correction gives wisdom,

but a child left to himself causes shame to his mother.

When the wicked increase, sin increases;

but the righteous will see their downfall.

Correct your son, and he will give you peace;

yes, he will bring delight to your soul.

Where there is no revelation, the people cast off restraint;

but one who keeps the law is blessed.

A servant can't be corrected by words.

Though he understands, yet he will not respond.

Do you see a man who is hasty in his words?

There is more hope for a fool than for him.

He who pampers his servant from youth

will have him become a son in the end.

An angry man stirs up strife,

and a wrathful man abounds in sin.

A man's pride brings him low,

but one of lowly spirit gains honor.

Whoever is an accomplice of a thief is an enemy of his own soul.

He takes an oath, but dares not testify.

The fear of man proves to be a snare,

but whoever puts his trust in the LORD is kept safe.

Many seek the ruler's favor,

but a man's justice comes from the LORD.

A dishonest man detests the righteous,

and the upright in their ways detest the wicked.

SEVENTY THREE

INSTRUCTIONS

> *"Where there is no revelation, the people
> cast off restraint; but one who keeps the law
> is blessed."* (PRO 29:18)

What is revelation? It is an insight from God. Wow! Imagine having access to someone who knows everything, sees everything, knows everyone, and can see into the future.

We absolutely have that with God, yet we tend to take it for granted. If you need some direction in your business, He is vitality interested in your work life. Imagine the opportunity to talk with the ultimate business guru. Would you go out of your way for an hour with Jobs or Gates? Well, you have access to someone far, far superior, better connected, and infinitely more capable. Why not spend some time with Him and get your revelation?

All leaders who profess Christ need to hear from Him. We operate in His Kingdom and have to play by His rules to be effective. In order to hear, we have to be close, there is no escape from the discipline and pleasure of spending time with Him. Expect opposition though, because it is your place of empowerment and revelation.

> **QUICK PRAYER**: I need Your revelation, Father.
> Amen.

CHAPTER 30

The words of Agur the son of Jakeh, the oracle:
the man says to Ithiel,
to Ithiel and Ucal:
"Surely I am the most ignorant man,
and don't have a man's understanding.
I have not learned wisdom,
neither do I have the knowledge of the Holy One.
Who has ascended up into heaven, and descended?
Who has gathered the wind in his fists?
Who has bound the waters in his garment?
Who has established all the ends of the earth?
What is his name, and what is his son's name, if you know?

"Every word of God is flawless.

He is a shield to those who take refuge in him.

Don't you add to his words,
lest he reprove you, and you be found a liar.

"Two things I have asked of you;
don't deny me before I die:
Remove far from me falsehood and lies.
Give me neither poverty nor riches.
Feed me with the food that is needful for me;
lest I be full, deny you, and say, 'Who is the LORD?'
or lest I be poor, and steal,
and so dishonor the name of my God.

SEVENTY FOUR

SHIELDED

"Every word of God is flawless. He is a shield
to those who take refuge in him." (PRO 30:5)

We all need protection. From time to time we are attacked. We are in a war; we should expect some flak. So how do we defend ourselves and fight back? Jesus used the Word of God as a weapon.

In this Scripture, we are advised to use God's Word as a shield. If you find yourself in trouble in business or in your personal life, speak the Word of God. Our organisations depend on us to protect and serve, both in the physical and in the spiritual; we have been given authority in both realms and need to be proficient in both.

Get to know your armory. You never know when you will need it. If you take the time to study the Bible, it will become a part of who you are. Speaking the Word was modeled to us by Jesus. How much more we need that protection!

QUICK PRAYER: Protect me when I need a shield, Lord. Teach me to use Your Word. Amen.

"Don't slander a servant to his master,

lest he curse you, and you be held guilty.

There is a generation that curses their father,

and doesn't bless their mother.

There is a generation that is pure in their own eyes,

yet are not washed from their filthiness.

There is a generation, oh how lofty are their eyes!

Their eyelids are lifted up.

There is a generation whose teeth are like swords,

and their jaws like knives,

to devour the poor from the earth, and the needy from among men.

"The leach has two daughters:

'Give, give.'

"There are three things that are never satisfied;

four that don't say, 'Enough:'

Sheol,

the barren womb;

the earth that is not satisfied with water;

and the fire that doesn't say, 'Enough.'

"The eye that mocks at his father,

and scorns obedience to his mother:

the ravens of the valley shall pick it out,

the young eagles shall eat it.

SEVENTY FIVE

SLANDER

"Don't slander a servant to his master,
lest he curse you, and you be held guilty."
(PRO 30:10)

There is something in human nature that finds satisfaction or even delight in gossip, slander, and having a good whine. Today take a listen to the conversations at work and see how often this is the case. If you want a shock, listen to how much you do it yourself.

There is a price we pay when we operate in this way and give into our human natures. It poisons our ability to see clearly regarding the person in question. Our insight and clarity diminish as we cloud out God's thoughts with the words we speak.

We also run a risk that others will repeat what we say and that it will eventually reach the ears of others. If we wish to be deemed trustworthy, we have to avoid slander so that it doesn't come back to get us.

> **QUICK PRAYER**: Keep me free of slander, Jesus. Amen.

"There are three things which are too amazing for me,
   four which I don't understand:
The way of an eagle in the air;
   the way of a serpent on a rock;
   the way of a ship in the midst of the sea;
   and the way of a man with a maiden.

"So is the way of an adulterous woman:
   she eats and wipes her mouth,
   and says, 'I have done nothing wrong.'

"For three things the earth tremble,
   and under four, it can't bear up:
For a servant when he is king;
   a fool when he is filled with food;
   for an unloved woman when she is married;
   and a handmaid who is heir to her mistress.

"There are four things which are little on the earth,
   but they are exceedingly wise:
   the ants are not a strong people,
   yet they provide their food in the summer.
The conies are but a feeble folk,
   yet make they their houses in the rocks.
The locusts have no king,
   yet they advance in ranks.
You can catch a lizard with your hands,
   yet it is in kings' palaces.

"There are three things which are stately in their march,
four which are stately in going:
The lion, which is mightiest among animals,
and doesn't turn away for any;
the greyhound,
the male goat also;
and the king against whom there is no rising up.

"If you have done foolishly in lifting up yourself,
or if you have thought evil,
put your hand over your mouth.
For as the churning of milk brings forth butter,
and the wringing of the nose brings forth blood;
so the forcing of wrath brings forth strife."

CHAPTER 31

The words of king Lemuel; the oracle which his mother taught him.

"Oh, my son!

Oh, son of my womb!

Oh, son of my vows!

Don't give your strength to women,

nor your ways to that which destroys kings.

It is not for kings, Lemuel;

it is not for kings to drink wine;

nor for princes to say, 'Where is strong drink?'

lest they drink, and forget the law,

and pervert the justice due to anyone who is afflicted.

Give strong drink to him who is ready to perish;

and wine to the bitter in soul:

Let him drink, and forget his poverty,

and remember his misery no more.

Open your mouth for the mute,

in the cause of all who are left desolate.

Open your mouth, judge righteously,

and serve justice to the poor and needy."

Who can find a worthy woman?

For her price is far above rubies.

The heart of her husband trusts in her.

He shall have no lack of gain.

She does him good, and not harm,

all the days of her life.

SEVENTY SIX

BIG MOUTH

*"Open your mouth for the mute, in the cause
of all who are left desolate."* (PRO 31:8)

If you are in a leadership position in business, God has given you influence. What will you use it for? To bless yourself and your family? Yes, that is fine. To bless others in your company or church? That is fine too. But what of those who have no voice in society, those who have no influence or resources—who will speak for them? How will their voice be heard and justice done?

Often we see life through our own worldview, blissfully unaware of others who are less fortunate than ourselves. It is our duty to look again and ask how we can help. You can make a difference. Is God speaking to you today?

QUICK PRAYER: Let me see the needs of others and have the courage to speak for them. Amen.

She seeks wool and flax,

and works eagerly with her hands.

She is like the merchant ships.

She brings her bread from afar.

She rises also while it is yet night,

gives food to her household,

and portions for her servant girls.

She considers a field, and buys it.

With the fruit of her hands, she plants a vineyard.

She arms her waist with strength,

and makes her arms strong.

She perceives that her merchandise is profitable.

Her lamp doesn't go out by night.

She lays her hands to the distaff,

and her hands hold the spindle.

She opens her arms to the poor;

yes, she extends her hands to the needy.

She is not afraid of the snow for her household;

for all her household are clothed with scarlet.

She makes for herself carpets of tapestry.

Her clothing is fine linen and purple.

Her husband is respected in the gates,

when he sits among the elders of the land.

She makes linen garments and sells them,

and delivers sashes to the merchant.

Strength and dignity are her clothing.

She laughs at the time to come.

She opens her mouth with wisdom.

SEVENTY SEVEN

BUSINESS WOMEN

> *"She considers a field, and buys it. With the fruit of her hands, she plants a vineyard."*
> (PRO 31:16)

Jesus was, and is, one of the greatest liberators of women in history— so much so that early writings see the 'Christian Way' as a political movement rather than a religious one. A key reason for this was the empowerment of women. In the society of the time, women were regarded as little more than chattels.

The clearest example we have of a great businessperson in the Bible is the Proverbs 31 woman. Here is a wonderful example of wisdom, application, diligence, and fiscal responsibility.

God is definitely into having women in business and leadership, so let's not get in His way with some of our religiosity. There is no glass ceiling in God's economy; He will exalt women into leadership roles if they allow Him to do so. Now is the time for women of God to rise up and take their full place in the marketplace.

QUICK PRAYER: I will honor women as You did, Jesus. Amen.

Faithful instruction is on her tongue.

She looks well to the ways of her household,

and doesn't eat the bread of idleness.

Her children rise up and call her blessed.

Her husband also praises her:

"Many women do noble things,

but you excel them all."

Charm is deceitful, and beauty is vain;

but a woman who fears the LORD, she shall be praised.

Give her of the fruit of her hands!

Let her works praise her in the gates!

MARK BILTON BSC. GRADDIPBUS. MBA. FAICD. FAIM

Mark Bilton is a, "Change Catalyst" with extensive Managing Director and CEO experience. He has led business transformation in many companies including, Gloria Jean's Coffees' global business, as Group Managing Director overseeing 40 countries.

Mark has led transformational change in many sectors, including importing, wholesale and retail. His leadership experience spans diverse industries; coffee, textiles, garments, appliances and consumer electronics.

He is internationally recognized for excellence in 'Change Management'. In 2011 he was awarded the "Young President's Organization's" prestigious "Terry Plochman Award" for global "Best of the Best". In 2014 he received the Michael Page 'Australian Retail Executive Award'.

Mark has served as an Independent Director on numerous 'not for profit', industry, leadership and commercial boards.

Mark has a passion for Christians in Business, and is the founder of 'Called to Business', who "encourage and equip Christians to be effective at work". He is also a speaker and the author of many books including "Monday Matters: Finding God in Your Workplace."

He is married to Helen, has three teenage children and lives in Sydney, Australia.

RECOMMENDED RESOURCES

Called to Business: www.CalledtoBusiness.com

Mark Bilton's online ministry to "Encourage and Equip Christians to be effective at Work." You will find many resources in this ministry, including a powerful weekly biblical business e-message that you can receive in your e-mail.

You can find Called to Business on the social media sites listed below:
www.Facebook.com/CalledtoBusiness
www.Twitter.com/Calledto

Mark Bilton: www.MarkBilton.com

Founder of Called to Business' Mark Bilton's personal blog.

You can find Mark Bilton on the social media sites listed below:
www.Facebook.com/MarkBilton
www.Twitter.com/MarkBilton
www.linkedin.com/in/markbilton
www.YouTube.com/MarkBilton
www.Google.com/+MarkBilton

OTHER RECOMMENDED MARKETPLACE MINISTRIES

www.**MarketplaceLeaders**.org

Os Hillman is president of Marketplace Leaders, an organization whose purpose is to help men and women discover and fulfill God's complete purposes through their work and to view their work as ministry. Marketplace Leaders exists to help men and women fulfill God's call on their lives by providing a *free* devotional that goes out to over a quarter of a million people all over the world and by training business leaders to see their work as a catalyst for change through training events and other ministry events.

www.**LICC**.org.uk

LICC exists to envision and equip Christians and their churches for whole-life missionary discipleship in the world. They seek to serve them with biblical frameworks, practical resources, training, and models so that they flourish as followers of Jesus and grow as whole-life disciple-making communities. Mark Greene is one of the most articulate and effective communicators in the marketplace today.

www.**GodatWork**.org.uk

In his book *God at Work*, Ken Costa writes about how the Christian faith should and can be lived out in day-to-day life at work. As a high-profile banker in the city of London, he considers the challenges of living out his faith at work and speaks openly of his own struggles with ambition, money, relationships, success, and failure.

By using the Biblical principles that underpin his faith and applying them to the 21st-century workplace of today, he offers practical advice on tackling the common problems familiar to many: the work-life balance, stress, ambition, failure, and disappointment.

www.**BusinessasMissionNetwork**.com

This is the most comprehensive source of information about the Business as Mission Movement, with many links to numerous companies, resources, and articles.

www.**EdSilvoso**.com

Ed Silvoso is one of the most effective marketplace ministers in the world, transforming many businesses and lives as he teaches comprehensively in many countries.

www.**JohnMaxwell**.com

John Maxwell is still one of the best and most-respected experts and teachers on leadership and personal growth.

MON✧AY
memos

A daily devotional for those in the workplace.

By Mark Bilton

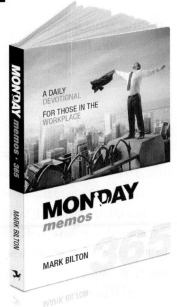

Does God really have a plan and a purpose for my work?

God is vitally, passionately, and intimately interested in the workplace. Many have embraced the biblical concept of our whole life being impacted by God, and that there is no separation between the sacred and the secular.

How do you integrate your faith with your work? Through real commercial experience, author Mark Bilton has walked with God and seen Him open doors that have taken him from the shop floor to the boardroom; from sales assistant to CEO.

In this book are 365 short, sharp, insightful messages that are scriptural and applicable to you and your work. They will transform your work life, and your workplace. There is no inconsistency between a Christian worldview and commercial success.

Work is a vital part of His plan and purpose for us. We have been lovingly crafted, anointed and appointed, for a particular purpose. We will only reach our full potential as we recognise God's hand at work in our work.

www.**MondayMemos**.com

MON?AY
matters

**Finding God in
your workplace.**

By Mark Bilton

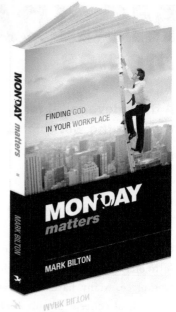

Is God really interested in my work?

There is a revolution taking place around the world. It is a realization that God is vitally, passionately, and intimately interested in the workplace. Many have embraced the biblical concept of our whole lives being impacted by God and that there is no separation between the sacred and the secular.

How do you find God in your workplace? In this book, Mark provides insights and a practical framework that lays out God's purpose for work. These lessons have been mined from real world commercial experience. Author Mark Bilton has walked with God and seen Him open doors that have taken him from the shop floor to the boardroom; from sales assistant to CEO.

Work is a vital part of His plan and purpose for us. We have been lovingly crafted, anointed, and appointed for a particular purpose. We will o nly reach our full potential as we recognize God's hand at work in our work.

www.**MondayMatters**.net

PRACTICE THE PRESENCE OF GOD

A CONTEMPORARY INTERPRETATION OF THE WORDS OF NICHOLAS HERMAN (BROTHER LAWRENCE c.1614-1691)

By Mark Bilton

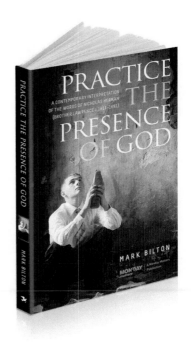

'The Practice of the Presence of God' is a venerated collection of conversations and letters that capture the wisdom of Nicholas Herman (Brother Lawrence). This fresh contemporary version will reach a new generation with his much-needed message.

The message is simple yet utterly profound. The discipline of being aware of God's presence and serving in utter reliance on Him is the core of what it means to be a follower of Jesus.

God has a plan and a purpose for your life; without exception, we are all anointed and appointed for a specific vocation. Take the simple message in this book and apply it to your life. You will find God in the midst of the exciting and mundane.

www.**BrotherLawrence**.org